To Kira,
who gave me time to write this book.

The Sanderson Collector's Unofficial Guide To
Sanderson Collecting

Mark Lindberg
Murphy Thomas
Foreword by Janci Patterson

Text copyright © 2024 by Mark Lindberg and Murphy Thomas

Foreword copyright © 2024 by Janci Patterson

Cover art and design © 2024 by Siena (Lotus) Buchanan

Zenef Mark glyph © 2021 by Isaac Stewart

Pictures by Mark Lindberg, Murphy Thomas, Kevin F. Dush, and Luke DeProst

This book is not official, licensed, authorized, or sponsored by Brandon Sanderson or Dragonsteel in any way.

All rights reserved.

ISBN 9798218547493

First Edition - December 5, 2024

0 9 8 7 6 5 4 3 2 1

book
koob

Table of Contents

Foreword..8
Introduction..10
Collecting Terminology...12
    Firsts (printings, editions, and states) and number lines......12
    ISBNs, and when they're not enough..................................15
    Types of collectible books..17
    Anatomy of a book...21
    Signed, lined, and dated...23
    Numbered and lettered..24
    Misprints..25
    Other common terminology...25
Care and Feeding of your Collection.......................................27
    Where to buy books..27
    What to look for when buying books..................................30
    Where and how to sell books..33
    Protecting books..35
    Cataloging books..38
Signed Sanderson Books..39
    Identifying Sanderson's signature......................................39
    Getting a signed book..41
    Bookplates...43
    Facsimile signatures: The Wheel of Time...........................43
    Sanderson-adjacent signatures..44
Collectible Books..51
Collectible Books - The Cosmere...52
    Elantris..52
    Mistborn..55
    The Stormlight Archive..72
    White Sand...91
    Other Planets...94
    Anthologies..102
Collectible Books - Non-Cosmere..105
    Star's End...105
    Alcatraz..106
    The Wheel of Time...114
    The Rithmatist..121

The Reckoners..122
The Cytoverse...127
Legion..135
Other - Fiction...140
Other - Nonfiction..150
Sanderson Swag Guide by Murphy Thomas.........................153
    SWAG "STUFF WE ALL GET".....................................153
    How to get it?..154
    Rare SWAG Guide..155
    Non book collectibles..157
    Foreign Edition SWAG..157
    Free Vs Purchased..158
    Crossover SWAG..158
Unicorns and Curiosities in my Personal Collection..............160
Afterword and Acknowledgments..167
Epilogue: A Longer Biography of The Sanderson Collector. .169

Foreword

Every author's dream is to be read. Better still than being read is to have your work be loved, and, in my opinion, there is no truer expression of love than collecting. To collect is a form of dedication, a consecration of space, money, resources, time, effort, and care to honoring something close to a person's heart. The value in a collection is far more than its worth on the market—the value of a collection is in the joy the collector finds in curating, storing, displaying, and sharing.

You can learn a lot about what a person values based on what they collect. Those who collect books and related memorabilia—who dedicate vast amounts of space and money and time to caring for, storing, and appreciating books and stories—build a legacy that not only shows how much they value literature but also preserve the legacy of that literature for the generations of readers who will come after.

I met Brandon Sanderson about a year before Elantris was published. At the time he was a disciplined and optimistic writer who wanted to make an indelible mark on the fantasy genre, but hadn't yet discovered how his work would be received. Sometimes I wish I could go back in time and tell my friend that he was going to do it. He was going to write fantasy that would speak to masses of people and change the way writers who came after him told their stories. If I could, I would describe to him the hundreds of people who would not only read his books and love his stories, but make collecting the books he wrote and produced a central part of their lives. It's that enthusiasm and fervor that truly speaks to me of how important Brandon's stories are to people, especially those who collect them.

In the labor of love that is Sanderson collecting, there is no greater source of knowledge than Mark Lindberg. Mark has not only built an impressive Sanderson collection, but also built a community around the practice of collecting itself. He is my personal go-to source of knowledge for all things collection-related, including tracking down hard-to-find copies of my own books (and so I will forgive him for pointing out in this book that I'm not the best at maintaining a consistent signature. Sorry collectors! Handwriting was always my worst subject in school.)

The book he's written is a great resource for all who want to express their love of Sanderson by collecting, and I hope it helps you to expand and care for your collection. Thank you for being a person who cares for and values books.

Most of all, thank you for reading.

-Janci Patterson

Introduction

Hello everyone, it's Mark. I am The Sanderson Collector. Over the past several years, I've collected as many Brandon Sanderson books as I could, and learned as much as I could about them and collecting in general. In this book, I'm going to share as much of that knowledge as I can, in hopes that it will be helpful to you.

Who am I? I'm one of Brandon's beta readers, and have been since the middle of 2015, when I beta read *Calamity* and *Mistborn: Secret History*. You can find me in the acknowledgments of nearly every book since then, in various forms.

In July 2018, I started a YouTube channel, calling myself "The Sanderson Collector", showing off my modest collection of Brandon Sanderson books. At the time, it was limited to almost all US and UK editions, mainly hardcovers with a smattering of paperbacks to fill things out. There were plenty of notable gaps in my collection. At the time, there was no central location for Sanderson Collectors to gather online. 17th Shard existed, but was mainly for chatting about the stories and theories. My videos became a place to meet and connect with other collectors.

In October 2018, I was contacted by Mike McDuffie about creating a Facebook group for Sanderson Collecting, in a similar vein to a Stephen King community he was a part of. I thought it was a great idea, and along with collector friend Luke DeProst, we created the first online community for Sanderson Collectors.

That Facebook group quickly grew past just viewers of my channel and, in July 2020, Greg Parker created a corresponding Discord server. I'll go into more detail on all of this in a later chapter, but in the interest of keeping this introduction brief, after a few years, this group morphed into the Sanderson Collectors Guild (SCG), of which I am a founding member and board member. I have worked at the guild booth at numerous conventions, worked hard to catalog books on a website created by another of our guild members, and generally been very active in the community.

Throughout it all, I have continued to run my YouTube channel as well as Instagram feed as The Sanderson Collector, as well as being an active part of the SCG.

My collection has grown over the years, and I now have what is indisputably the largest Brandon Sanderson book collection in the world.

I have a nearly complete collection of ARCs, as well as over 1,000 distinct editions and printings of his many books in over 30 languages. I have an extensive knowledge of many aspects of collecting, and I love sharing this knowledge with friends and fellow fans.

Therefore, I am writing this book to put it all in one place, collecting it for easy reference. I hope that you find it a helpful guide on your journey through collecting books. The first part of this book is an introduction to collecting terminology and methods, and care of valuable books. The second part delves directly into Sanderson's books, detailing values and differences between editions. It is my hope that the first part can serve as a general collecting guide and will be useful to any book collector, no matter what books you collect. And the second part can serve as the most detailed and comprehensive guide to everything Collecting Sanderson.

I have worn many hats over the years. Fan. Beta reader. Social media personality. SCG founder and archivist. Educator. And now, writer. It is my hope that you find something useful and interesting in these pages.

Happy Collecting.

-- Mark Lindberg, Fall 2024

Collecting Terminology

Like many hobbies, book collecting has its own lingo, which can be nearly indecipherable to an outsider. Understanding the common terminology is essential if you want to know what books other collectors are selling or looking for, and to help you figure out what kind of book you have and what it is worth. In addition, understanding the terminology and the types of collectible books can help you narrow down your focus, and decide which books you want to collect.

Firsts (printings, editions, and states) and number lines

Most collectors want the earliest published copies of a book. This means that they are searching out the first state of the first printing of the first edition of that book, and usually the hardcover or an Advance Reader's Copy (ARC). They identify most of this information via the number line on the copyright page. There's a lot to break down in those sentences, so let's go over it one term at a time.

The **copyright page** is the page (or pages in rare cases), usually found behind the title page near the front of a book, that has all the technical copyright information about the book. It will have the number line, the ISBN and Library of Congress cataloging information, the publisher's information, and if it's fiction, the disclaimer about similarities to real people being coincidental. It can hold any other info that the publisher wishes to include, and I've seen a wide variety over the years.

The **number line** is a line of numbers, typically found on the copyright page of a book, that tells you the printing of a book. It is often found near or at the bottom of the copyright page. Not all copyright pages have a number line, some instead simply state the printing.

The **printing** of a book is determined by the entire print run that the publisher orders from the printer. They will typically store these books in a warehouse, and when the print run is getting close to sold out, they order a new print run of the book, and it becomes the next printing.

The **state** of a book changes anytime anything other than the number line changes. If the dust jacket price changes, the state changes. If the bibliography list at the front of the book changes, the state changes. If the publisher fixes a typo in the text of the book, the state changes. States are numbered, so you look for the first state, second state, and so on. Usually, but with notable exceptions, the state only changes between printings of a book. Unlike printings and editions, which are defined and listed by the publisher, the state of a book is only determined and numbered by the collecting community.

The **edition** of a book is all copies of a book that are similar enough that the publisher says they are the same, always within the same format, typically with the same ISBN, and the same sequence of printings. Details may change within an edition. Typically, these are things that change the state of a book, like cover price, formatting of text on the cover, and typo fixes. Occasionally, there are large changes like the cover art of a book within the same edition, which can get confusing when cataloging and identifying editions. It is relatively rare to have a second edition in the same format.

When a book is released in a new format, for example going from hardcover to trade paperback, the new format is typically called the "first edition thus". Therefore, we get first edition hardcovers, first edition trade paperbacks, first edition mass market paperbacks, and so on. Each edition will start from the first printing of that edition (and the first state) and the numbers will increase from there.

Collectors will often refer to a book as a 1/1. This means it is the first edition, first printing of that book. The first edition, second printing would be a 1/2. The second edition, first printing would be a 2/1. If there are states that are relevant within a printing, such as with the leatherbound *The Way of Kings*, we refer to the book as a 1/1/1, with the last number representing the state.

In order to identify the edition/printing/state of a book, there are a few things to look for. The copyright page usually holds almost all of the relevant information. The number line will tell you which printing a book is by the lowest number. If the number line has a 0, that represents a 10, so you ignore it. The pictures below show a first printing and a seventh printing, respectively.

> Printed in the United States of America
> 10 9 8 7 6 5 4 3 2 1
> First Edition

> Printed in the United States of America
>
> 0 9 8 7

In some books, most commonly UK books, the number line is written in an alternating format. The printing is still determined by the lowest number on that line, whether it is on the left or the right. The pictures below show a first and a second printing UK book.

> 1 3 5 7 9 10 8 6 4 2
>
> Printed in Great Britain by
> Clays Ltd, St Ives plc

> 3 5 7 9 10 8 6 4 2
>
> Printed in Great Britain by Clays Ltd, St Ives plc

Other publishers have done away with the number line altogether. You see this most commonly with translated books, such as the Spanish editions. They will instead either omit printing information (quite frustrating) or in a straightforward manner state which printing or reprint the book is.

Shown below are a UK 21st printing, and a Spanish fourth printing (Tercera reimpresión = third reprint).

> This Orbit edition published in 1991
> Reprinted 1991, 1992 (twice), 1993 (twice),
> 1994 (twice), 1995, 1996 (twice), 1997, 1998, 1999, 2000,
> 2001, 2002 (twice), 2003, 2004 (twice)

> Título original: *The Well of Ascension: Book Two of Mistborn*
>
> Primera edición en este sello: septiembre de 2021
> Tercera reimpresión: diciembre de 2022

Additionally, the copyright page will often say what edition the book is. A line like "First hardcover edition 2010" or "First Mass Market Edition 2013" will tell you that a book is the first edition thus. Later editions, which are relatively rare, will have a line such as "Second hardcover edition 2014" or will have two lines, one for the first edition, and one for this later edition, stating when they were first published.

On occasion, these additional lines will be omitted, and a second edition will simply state when it was first published. In these cases, you should check a guide for which edition is the first edition thus.

Print-on-demand books typically do not have a number line. They will sometimes have a barcode in the back with a little note about when and where the book was printed up. Because they can be printed in any amount at any time, there are no official "first printings" of print-on-demand books.

There is no official indication in the book for the state of the book, however. That is a term defined and identified purely by collectors. We get several copies of a book, and do detailed comparisons of the contents and packaging, looking for any differences we can use to identify the books. In most cases, this is something like the cover price of the book changing, but on other occasions can be as subtle as a fix for a typo on one page of the book.

In order to identify the state of a book, consult the existing collecting community's knowledge. For many authors, this knowledge is contained among several related or unrelated webpages, and in some cases, isn't even publicly available, instead requiring you to be "in the know" with other members of the collecting community.

In the Sanderson collecting community, we do our best to make this knowledge as easily and widely available as possible. When there is an interesting distinction between states of a book, especially if they're in the same printing, I try to make a video explaining the differences. In addition, we maintain the collectingsanderson.com website, which attempts to detail all known differences between the states of any Sanderson book.

Being able to identify the state of a book based on the dust jacket -- for example from a price change or which review is quoted on the back -- is a valuable skill. In many cases, it will allow you to pick out a first printing book from an online listing without needing to ask the seller for a picture of the copyright page, meaning nobody else will buy the book while you're waiting for a response.

ISBNs, and when they're not enough

International Serial Book Numbers (ISBNs) are the little barcode numbers you find on the back of nearly every book. They are meant to be unique for every edition of a book, although there are plenty of cases where this is not true. For example, book club editions have the same ISBN as the original hardcover, and ARCs typically share that ISBN as well.

In addition, ISBNs do not tell you the printing or state of a book. For a single edition, the ISBN will always remain the same, even as the printing or state changes. When you are attempting to collect a 1/1 of a book, you cannot rely on just the ISBN. You must check the copyright page to determine the printing, and in a few cases, other pages as well to determine the state of the book.

Other notable examples of ISBNs not being enough in Sanderson books include the UK *Oathbringer* mass market paperbacks, where Gollancz reissued the books with a different spine color but still called them a 1/1 mass market paperback, and the UK *The Way of Kings* split hardcovers, where Gollancz reissued the books with reflowed text, and also called them a 1/1 of that format.

Some books, like the US first edition mass market paperback of *Mistborn*, change cover art between printings, meaning the Chris McGrath Vin cover and the Jon Foster Grim Reaper cover share the same ISBN, while the Grim Reaper cover is collectible and the Vin cover is not. *The Rithmatist* US young adult paperback has also changed covers in the same ISBN, though neither version is collectible.

ISBNs were historically 10-digit numbers, but now are always 13-digit numbers. They nearly always start with the numbers 978. ISBN-13s are a specific form of an EAN (European Article Number), the number used for the barcode you will find on nearly anything you can buy at a store. The first 3 digits of an EAN tell you which country an item is from. In the case of books, the 978 is for a fictional country called "Bookland".

No, I'm not making that up. All books are from Bookland.

For some more recent books, although no Sanderson books that I have seen, the ISBN will start with 979, which also denotes Bookland. This is because 978 ISBNs are starting to run out, and eventually, I believe many books will have a 979 ISBN.

Books published before 2007 was originally issued with just a 10-digit ISBN. All of these 10-digit ISBNs can be retroactively turned into 13-digit ISBNs by addition of the 978 prefix and recalculation of the final digit, as that digit is a checksum of the rest of the number. However, you cannot rely upon only that ISBN, as there can be a 978 and a 979 book with the same last 10 digits that are completely different books. Only ISBN-13s should be used when buying and selling books.

While every book published by a major publisher since 1967 will have an ISBN, not every single collectible does. For example, ARCs and ABMs typically do not have ISBNs, nor do magazines or promotional items, and some books not from a major publisher, like *Altered Perceptions*, simply do not have an ISBN.

If you want more information on ISBNs in general, the Wikipedia article on the subject is detailed and comprehensive, and I highly recommend it.

Types of collectible books

Books run the gamut from being worth well over 50 times the original cover price of the book to being worth half the price, and much of that depends on the format. The most common formats are explained below.

Hardcovers

Hardcovers are your bread and butter collectible. In the vast majority of cases, they are the first book that is published for a general release, and the 1/1 of the hardcover is what most collectors will want. They are bound with hard boards at the end of the book, and typically have a dust jacket around the boards. The vast majority of Sanderson books have a hardcover edition.

In a few rare cases, such as *The Emperor's Soul*, the hardcover is not actually the first printing, but is still highly collectible.

Leatherbounds

Leatherbound books are hardcover books bound in leather. They are typically the most deluxe edition of a book, and often include additional art, full color illustrations, forewords, or deleted scenes, and can be worth a lot. Every Sanderson leatherbound is collectible and discussed in detail in the Identification Guide.

Dragonsteel, the company that Sanderson runs which produces almost all of his swag and special editions, has released leatherbound editions of many of Sanderson's Cosmere works, and signed (especially numbered) first editions of all of them command a hefty price tag.

Sanderson's *The Wheel of Time* books also have numbered and lettered leatherbound editions, although those do not have any additional artwork.

Deluxe Editions

Deluxe editions, almost always hardcovers, are books put out in addition to the regular hardcover released by the publisher. They have special features, often additional artwork or sprayed edges, to enhance them from the baseline books. However, they are bound with cloth boards, and are often slightly lower quality (binding, etc.) compared to leatherbounds. In Sanderson collecting, these often come as Dragonsteel editions.

Dragonsteel has released deluxe editions of all of the secret project books, as well as *The Way of Kings Prime* and *Dragonsteel Prime*. These deluxe editions are all casewrapped, and the secret project books include numerous pieces of art, as well as two-color text.

In addition, there are several sprayed edge editions from various sources, mainly Gollancz (the publisher) and Waterstones (a bookstore) in the UK.

Some foreign language editions, such as the Bulgarian *Cytoverse* books and the Spanish *Mistborn* books, have very cool deluxe editions.

The only high-value deluxe edition at the time of writing is the 1/1 of *The Way of Kings Prime*. All other Dragonsteel editions are still available on their website, the sprayed edge editions haven't been rare enough, and none of the translated editions are sought after highly enough to command high prices. We are getting a reprint of *The Way of Kings Prime* with the *Words of Radiance* BackerKit rewards, and that book has a new cover design, making it a second edition. The first printing will be a 2/1. This has already seen the price of the 1/1 drop by nearly half, and we don't even have the new books yet.

Book Club Editions (BCEs)

Book club editions, often abbreviated as BCEs, are editions published by a book club, usually the Science Fiction Book Club, in hardcover on low quality paper. Many, but not all, of them are smaller than the original hardcover. They do not have a number line on the copyright page, and always include the book club number in a small white box somewhere on the back cover of the book.

BCEs will usually have the same ISBN as the original book, despite being a separate edition.

Be wary of these in online listings. There are no collectible/valuable book club editions of Sanderson books. Always check for that little box with the number on the back, and the lack of a number line on the copyright page.

Library Editions

Library editions, or library binding books, are hardcovers that are bound specifically for use in libraries. These books do not have a dust jacket, instead being casewrapped, meaning the cover art is printed directly onto the boards. Without a dust jacket that can tear, these books are much more durable, which is what makes them highly desirable for libraries.

In some cases, these books are simply rebound copies of existing paperbacks or hardcovers. The company Turtleback Books started this trend, and released many editions in this format. They later scaled back their business, and no longer sell publicly, instead only marketing to public libraries and educational institutions.

In all cases that I have seen with Sanderson books, library editions will have their own ISBN.

There are no collectible/valuable library editions of Sanderson books.

Paperbacks

Paperbacks are books with flexible paper for the ends, instead of hard boards. They come in a variety of shapes and sizes, and nearly every book has various paperback editions, which are typically released one to three years after the initial hardcover release.

Although paperback sizes can vary widely, there are three common formats: trade paperbacks, young adult paperbacks, and mass market paperbacks.

Trade paperbacks (TPBs) are the same size and layout as the hardcover edition of the book, and are generally floppy. For the *Stormlight* books, we get these about one year after the release of the hardcover. Many books, including almost all Sanderson books outside of *Stormlight* and *Mistborn*, never get a trade paperback, excepting the international trade paperback.

Mass market paperbacks (MMPBs) are the short, squat books that you most commonly see at the bookstore, especially at used bookstores. They are a very standard size, and typically come out one to two years after the initial book. All of Sanderson's Tor titles older than two or three years have MMPBs.

The only collectible Sanderson MMPBs are *Armored*, an anthology that is only available in that format and is the first publication of *HARRE*, the Grim Reaper cover of *Mistborn*, and the *Mistborn/The Way of Kings* sampler.

Young adult paperbacks (YA PBs) sit in the middle ground, being smaller than TPBs, but slightly taller and deeper than MMPBs. They are released almost exclusively for young adult titles. All of Sanderson's Delacorte titles have YA PBs instead of MMPBs, and Mistborn Era One has a YA PB treatment by Tor Teen. None of these editions are collectible.

The list of other collectible Sanderson paperbacks includes *The Emperor's Soul*, *Writing Fantasy Heroes*, *Infinity Blade*, and *Cardinalities*, all of which are discussed in detail in the identification and pricing guide. None of these books are strictly trade paperbacks, but all are larger than mass market size.

While they are not regular paperbacks, there are a number of sampler booklets and promotional pamphlets for Sanderson's various works, and there isn't a better category to put them in. None of these is super sought after (except maybe before the book itself is released), so none are listed in the identification and pricing guide.

Magazines

Magazines are regular publications that you subscribe to, and often contain a collection of short stories and essays by various authors. They are almost always small paperbacks printed on cheap paper, and often have a mailing label directly attached to them. There are a handful of magazines that have Sanderson stories in them, and they can include some of the more rare and cool collectibles.

ARCs and ABMs

Advance Reader Copies (ARCs) and Advance Bound Manuscripts (ABMs) are copies of a book that are printed up in limited quantities before the book is officially published, and may not contain the final text or artwork for the book. ARCs are sent out to bookstores and book reviewers to generate hype for the book, and are often marked with "NOT FOR SALE" on the cover.

ABMs are slightly different from ARCs in that they have an even earlier version of the text, without the proper fonts or typesetting, and are sent out to other authors for review and to gather cover quotes to put on the final book. They are even more rare than ARCs.

ARCs can go by a handful of different names, some of which blur the line between ARC and ABM. I have seen Advance Reading Copy, Advance Uncorrected Proof, Advance Proof Copy, Uncorrected Advance Reading Copy, Advanced Reader's Copy, and more. The key words to look for are some form of "advance" or "proof".

Despite never being officially sold, there is a massive demand and market for these books, and many collectors consider them the pinnacle of collecting a specific book, because it is the truly first released edition of the book, and is also very limited in quantity. There are often only 100-200 copies of the ARC or ABM of a book printed, sometimes as low as 25-50.

Some books can have multiple ARCs, from the UK and the US, or across multiple rereleases of the book. In this case, we distinguish which edition of the ARC we are talking about with other identifiers. Examples of this with Sanderson books include ARCs for each reissue of *Alcatraz Versus the Evil Librarians*, as well as US and UK ARCs for *Steelheart*.

Only the early Sanderson books have ABMs. After a certain point, Sanderson became popular enough that he didn't need the additional cover quotes, plus his publishing schedule became tight enough that ABMs stopped being feasible. Every Sanderson ABM is highly collectible and valuable.

Additionally, nearly every Sanderson ARC is as well. Notable exceptions being *Bastille vs. the Evil Librarians*, where a very high number of ARCs were printed, and being the sixth book in one of Sanderson's less popular series, the demand is low. The price is not much higher than the hardcover of the book. *Steelheart* (US ARC with cover art) is in a similar boat. It, and *The Rithmatist* and *Skyward* ARCs aren't more than a few hundred dollars, sometimes less if you find the right deal. Anything Cosmere, on the other hand, is in high demand.

Anatomy of a book

Books are more complicated than you might initially realize, with different editions having all kinds of different features. The things that any book will have in common, however, are the cover and the page block.

The **cover** is whatever is around the outside of the book, whether it be hard boards, paper, or in a few special cases, wood. It will typically at least have the name of the book on it.

The **page block** is the pages that contain the actual book. They are lined up and cut into a rectangular solid by the printer, this solid being called the "block".

Page blocks are made up of **signatures**, sections of 16 pages that are printed together. In the printing process, 16 pages of a book are printed onto one large sheet of paper, which is then folded on itself 4 times, then cut, to form the 16 separate pages. You can often see these groups of 16 pages when you look at the top and bottom of a page block near the spine, especially on sewn editions. Signatures (which are not to be confused with signed books) are why so many misprints involve multiples of 16 pages.

Some books, especially print-on-demand books, do not have signatures. Instead, the pages are all printed individually, and then glued into the spine of the book.

The **spine** of a book is the back part that holds up the page block, and is what you typically see when books are lined up on the shelf. The spine is nearly always the part of the cover that is guaranteed to have the title on it, even on books that simply have a symbol on the front, such as *The Way of Kings Prime*, or any of the naked *Stormlight* books under the dust jacket.

The part of the page block directly opposite the spine is called the **fore edge**, and is the most common place for sprayed or painted edges.

The edges of a page block are usually completely flat. However, for aesthetic reasons, some books have uneven page edges on the fore edge. These are called **deckled edges**. I personally dislike them because they make it a lot harder to flip through the book one page at a time, but they have their fans. The only Sanderson books I can think of with deckled edges are the numbered editions of the Unfettered anthologies.

On a hardcover book, the **boards** are the hard pieces that make up the front and the back. Typically, these are some form of compressed cardboard, wrapped with cloth or leather. In a few rare cases (some Bulgarian editions), they are actual wood.

The **endpapers** are the pieces of paper at the front and back of a book that are glued to the boards. These are what hold the boards to the page block, and they often have art on them. They are typically printed on thicker paper than the rest of the book.

The **dust jacket** is the piece of paper that is placed over the boards of a hardcover book, and has the cover art printed on it. These slide right off of a book, and if they are in the same state (same price, same placement of text, etc.) are interchangeable between hardcover books. It is a common practice to find a very nice, maybe signed, 1/1 of a book with a beat up or missing dust jacket, and get another copy with an identical dust jacket -- maybe a cheaper unsigned copy of the same printing, or maybe a slightly later printing where nothing changed -- just to take the dust jacket off and put it with the more valuable edition.

The **headband** is the little piece of fabric, usually colorful, that sticks up above and below the page block right at the spine of the book. These days it is a purely decorative piece of fabric, but historically the books were sewn onto a piece of cloth for the binding, and the excess of that cloth would be the headband. Sometimes the headband at the bottom is called the **footband**, but often it is also still referred to as the headband.

A book where the pages are glued to the spine is called **glued**. Glued books are typically cheaper and faster to produce. Even books with signatures can be glued, with chunks of 16 pages glued together and then glued to the backing. All paperbacks are glued.

On the other hand, if thread is used to secure the pages to the backing or spine of a book, the book is **sewn**. Many deluxe editions are sewn, as it provides a nicer book that will lay open more easily, has a spine that won't crack with repeated use, and is considerably more durable.

Note that most regular hardcovers are glued, even though the pages will typically be grouped into signatures. You can tell this by looking at the top of the book where the spine meets the page block, and seeing the glue holding the sections in place.

Some books have a **ribbon bookmark**, a little ribbon that is sewn or glued to the binding of the book, and can be used to mark your place.

Signed, lined, and dated

A **signed book** is a book that has a signature in it from someone who contributed to the making of the book. Signed books often command a premium on the collecting market. The value of the signature can vary from book to book, and also depends on who signed the book. In most cases, we're talking about the author of the book signing it, but I have seen plenty of books signed by the cover artist as well, and I know plenty of people who collect books signed by all the people in the acknowledgments, though they tend to get these signed personally, and they're not something that really goes up for sale.

Artist signatures tend to be rare enough that pricing them is hard. Some people will not want the book if it is signed by anyone but the author, but plenty of people will want artist signed copies. Artists vary wildly in ease of access. Howard Lyon and Steve Argyle, for example, live near Sanderson and attend his convention every year, and are happy to sign stacks of books. Isaac Stewart and Ben McSweeney are generally very accessible as well.

Other artists, such as Ernanda Souza and Nabetse Zitro in *The Sunlit Man*, don't even live in the United States, and the only way to get a book signed by them is to message them, get their address, ship your book to them, have them sign it, pay for them to ship it back, and hope that it doesn't get damaged in transit. These signatures are significantly rarer.

When Sanderson signs a book, he will sometimes add something in addition to the signature. When he writes a person's name in the book, that's called **personalization**. I have several books personalized to "Mark", and they are my reading copies. For most collectors (except my friend Wolves), this devalues the book, and may be a deal breaker at any price for some people.

However, if you have a personalization slot, Sanderson may instead write a quote from the book and the current date, without adding a name. The quote from the book is called a **line**, and the date is a **date**, making the book "signed, lined, and dated". These books tend to be slightly more expensive than a plain signed book, especially if the date is close to the book's original release date.

Numbered and lettered

Sometimes, when a book is released, there will be a limited run of **numbered** copies. These books are numbered starting at #1, and going up. The number of copies varies depending on the book. Some books like Subterranean Press editions, have a fixed small number of numbered copies, and are numbered on a special page at the front of the book, which says how many numbered copies there are in total.

Other times, Sanderson will sign a bunch of regular copies of a book for release, and these copies will typically be sold for the release party. In the early years, this was done through Weller Books, and occasionally Sanderson would number more books for the release signings on subsequent days. In more recent years, these books are sold through Dragonsteel themselves, and a set number are reserved for the people present at the release party, with higher numbers going to people who order online.

Starting in 2020 with *Rhythm of War*, the release party numbered books that come from Dragonsteel have a stamp in addition to the number. This is excellent for the collectors, because it means that we can trust that someone didn't simply get a signed 1/1 copy of a book and write in the number themselves. There is no absolute way to verify books that aren't numbered with a stamp or tip-in page.

With the most recent releases -- *Defiant* and *Wind and Truth* -- Dragonsteel has started a new practice. Now if you want a numbered book on release, you must buy a "book bundle" which includes the book as well as various swag items such as pins, bookmarks, or other items, whether or not you want these items. This has raised the price of the numbered books significantly, up to three times the cover price of the book, which makes collecting them more difficult.

Lower numbers are more valuable, up to a point. The one- and two-digit numbers for a book are extra valuable, with number 1 being incredibly sought after. For the release party book releases, people have the opportunity to line up overnight and get their number early the next morning. It is common for people to line up for 12 hours or more, in freezing weather, in order to get number 1. The person who got number 1 for *A Memory of Light* lined up and camped out in a tent for a week before the release of the book in order to get the first number.

In addition to numbered books, some specialty presses release lettered editions. These editions are lettered A-Z, and sometimes come with extra perks, like slipcases or traycases. In some cases, the publisher will do a double set, lettering the next 26 books with AA-ZZ. In the case of *Snapshot*, the short-lived Vault Books even did a 3rd set, lettering AAA-ZZZ, for a total of 78 lettered editions. In all cases, these books are more rare than the numbered editions, and command a correspondingly high price tag.

In both cases, a publisher may sometimes produce "PC" books, where PC stands for Publisher's Copy. The "PC" is put in the place of the number or letter. Typically these books are extras produced either to give to friends of the publisher/author, or are extras in case damaged copies need to be replaced, and are often sold at charity auctions years after the book's release.

Misprints

Misprints are books that had a mistake or error during the printing process. They are not **damaged books**, which are books where the damage happens after the printing process, like the cover being torn off or the spine broken. Misprints come in a wide variety.

I personally think misprints are very cool and unique, and I collect them. I am in the minority in this case, though, and for most people a misprint isn't much different from a damaged book.

Some interesting misprints I have collected include: A *Skyward* ARC with a set of 16 pages missing; a *The Well of Ascension* leatherbound with the entire book bound in upside down; a *The Way of Kings* MMPB where the pages were misaligned and some of the signatures didn't get cut; a *The Way of Kings* US Hardcover with a set of pages from *Lord of Chaos* in the middle; a set of secret project books with bizarre foiling issues on the covers; an *Elantris* leatherbound with blue ink stains on various pages; a *Words of Radiance* trade paperback with an entire section repeated; and a paperback tip-in signed *Cytonic* where Sanderson's signature is cut in half.

If you come across a cool misprint of one of Sanderson's books, and it is not something you want to collect, please message me! In most cases, I'm happy to buy you a replacement copy (assuming I can get it for you at close to cover price) and pay you to ship your copy to me.

Other common terminology

Remainder marks are small dots made with a permanent marker on the edge of a book's pages. They denote that the book was marked as unsold by the bookstore, and they didn't pay the publisher for it. These marks are unsightly, and will heavily devalue a book. In some cases, people have had success sanding off the marks to refurbish a book, but it can be a tricky process, so don't attempt this without careful consideration, as you could easily damage the book and further devalue it.

When Sanderson travels, he will often stop at bookstores along the way, especially in airports, and sign whatever copies they have of his books. These books are called **Brandalized** books. If Sanderson posts on social media about the books, they're inevitably gone within a few hours, or even minutes if the store will ship orders.

Some books are not signed directly. Instead, Sanderson will sign a sheet of paper, which is then glued into the already finished book. This signed piece of paper is called a **tip-in**. Tip-in signed books are generally less valuable than those signed on the title page, with exceptions for editions like the Barnes and Noble numbered editions that come with the release of some books.

Some special edition books will come with a slipcase or a traycase. A **slipcase** is a box for a book to sit in on the shelf that is open on one side, letting the spine of the book show. The book can be slipped out by simply tilting the slipcase. A **traycase** is an enclosed box that folds over the entire book, and must be pulled off the shelf and opened fully to get the book out. Often, but not always, slipcases are for numbered books, and traycases are for the lettered editions.

Care and Feeding of your Collection

Now you know all about the different types of collectible books. You understand what other collectors mean when they talk about books. You might have a few books in your collection, you might have an idea of which books you want to go out and collect. Awesome! Now you need to know where to go to feed (grow) your collection, how to be safe doing it, and how to take care of all those awesome books you have. This part covers all of that.

Where to buy books

There are a lot of places where you can buy books. The primary one is, obviously, your local bookstore. If that's not an option, places like Amazon, Barnes and Noble's webstore, or bookshop.org are great alternatives. For Sanderson books, Dragonsteel Books' website is also a great place to shop. While all of these are great place to buy a book for reading, none of them is a good place to go to find specific collectible editions, though most will get you a 1/1 copy of a book upon release. Standard bookstores will sell whatever the latest printing of a book is, and they will often ship them loose in a box, meaning they'll arrive at your doorstep at least slightly damaged.

If you want a specific older edition, however, you will need to hunt down books on the secondary market. There are a number of places you can go, and a lot of things to watch out for.

eBay, AbeBooks, Mercari

eBay, AbeBooks, and Mercari are going to be your go-to websites for finding used and collectible copies of books. Mercari is especially nice, as they require every listing to have user-taken pictures of the actual item being sold, so there's a much higher chance you can see the copyright page, and you can tell at a glance which edition it is.

AbeBooks has its own nice features. The most important one is that they only sell books, so their listings require some specific info about the book. In particular, this includes the ISBN, so you can quickly use the ISBN on a book to narrow down a search and save it.

eBay is the biggest market on the list. More used Sanderson books and items go through eBay than everywhere else online combined, and so by sheer volume, you're more likely to find books you want here. Sellers also tend to know that eBay will have the largest pool of buyers, and will often put more valuable books up for auction.

All three sites have good return and refund policies for buyers, especially Mercari. Still, always carefully review the seller's description and pictures, because in order to be able to have a valid return, you'll need to show that the item received somehow does not match what the seller claimed. This is more important with sellers though AbeBooks, as they allow listings without pictures. If there is a problem with a book that you have bought, you'll need to contact the seller or the site you bought it through, and attempt to get it fixed. There is no reason for you to lose your money if they did not deliver what was promised.

If the seller doesn't have the specific pictures you need, in order to verify that the book is a 1/1, doesn't have a remainder mark, etc., message them and ask! I have found that, outside of the very large stores on eBay, almost everyone will respond with the pictures you ask for. The only risk here is that someone else may buy the listing before you do, but unless it's a super rare book like Infinity Blade, more copies will come by if you're patient. It's better to be safe than sorry when you can.

With online sellers, it can be hit or miss if they will properly package the rare books. If you can contact the seller, it never hurts to message them when you buy the book, let them know that it is an important book to you, and ask that they ship it safely. Sellers generally want to make you happy (so that they get good feedback, be sure to leave that feedback), and so these are not unreasonable requests.

AbeBooks and eBay allow you to save searches, and will send you an email when a listing comes up that matches your search terms. eBay will only send the email once a day, so it's very bad if you're trying to find deals on sought after books. However, it's better than nothing, and I have saved searches on both sites.

As a small addendum to this section, Amazon does have a used section for books online. It can be a real pain trying to narrow down which edition/ISBN you want, as Amazon has an absolutely horrible interface for this. Also, you will almost never find any user-uploaded pictures of editions on here. However, you may rarely find one with a description stating it is a first printing in like-new condition, and Amazon also has a very good return policy. You may also message sellers, especially if they're smaller sellers, to ask for a picture of the copyright page of the book they are selling. More often than not, they will respond.

Dragonsteel Books

Dragonsteel Books is a bit of a misnomer sometimes. Prior to the COVID-19 epidemic, they did sell a lot of books, including most of Sanderson's hardcovers, signed, in the latest printings. However, as Sanderson's popularity has continued to grow, it became infeasible for them to keep all of these books in stock, and so they simply stopped offering them, and now offer more merch and swag than actual books.

They still offer signed and numbered books upon the release of almost every new book, excluding secret projects. These books typically go up for sale around one to two months before the release date of the book.

In addition to this, they are the only place to buy new copies of the leatherbound books. While leatherbounds will go up for sale on used sites, Dragonsteel will sell them new, and they ship all their books safely. These books will be whatever the latest printing is, and will not always be signed (something that makes me very sad for the deluxe editions), but it is often the best price you can get. If you read the fine print on the Dragonsteel store, they will tell you what printing you are buying.

Leatherbound books are gorgeous regardless of printing, and if you're looking for the prettiest books at the lowest prices for your shelves, you cannot go wrong with ordering the leatherbounds through Dragonsteel.

None of the new books or product drops through Dragonsteel come unannounced these days, so I highly recommend at least vaguely following their social medias if you want to be aware of when the books will drop. Depending on the book, these drops can sell out fairly quickly, so it's often a good idea to set an alarm for the release of new books, and set aside some time in case there are technical issues. With the Mistborn Era Two leatherbounds, the website got stuck putting people in a queue that never actually let them get the book, and all of the numbered editions *sold out in under six minutes*. When the Words of Radiance Leatherbound BackerKit launched, the entire website went down for nearly an hour before any orders could be made. Be ready for technical troubles with websites when the Sanderson fanbase is involved, and be ready for things to sell very quickly.

Used Bookstores

Used bookstores can be a complete waste of time, but they can also turn up unexpected treasures. Numerous people in the collectors guild have found books ranging from numbered leatherbounds to first printings of early Cosmere novels, for cover price or even less, in used bookstores.

They are a great place to pick up *Wheel of Time* hardcovers as well, if you're collecting a set of those, especially a second set for the Juniper dust jackets. Most bookstores I have been to will have several of these, and usually at low prices. With a bit of patience, you can collect first printings of all except maybe the first five books in the series for very low prices. If you're looking for a set to put the Juniper dust jackets on, your selection becomes even bigger, as copies without dust jackets are common.

My personal favorite (because it's the most common near me) used bookstore is the chain Half Price Books. There are plenty of other options, though, and I recommend searching for used bookstores in your area to find out what there is. I do this whenever I'm traveling and have extra time, as my local bookstores tend to be picked over, and it's more likely I'll find something new and exciting at a new-to-me used bookstore.

SCG

The Sanderson Collectors Guild (SCG) has grown to be a big community online, with several thousand members in both the Discord server and the Facebook group. There are places on both groups to buy and sell collectible books.

You won't find tons of books listed in either place, but sales posts do pop up fairly regularly, and people there know what they have, and what a fair sale price is. In general, they will not try to scam you, and play nicely when trading. However, with all personal trades, I highly recommend paying with buyer protection such as PayPal's Goods and Services, not Friends and Family.

This is also a good place to post a looking-for advertisement. Many collectors have extra copies of some things, or at least copies they'd be willing to sell for the right price. Even if they don't have exactly what you're looking for, they will often be happy to keep their eyes open for a copy for you, and let you know if they have seen one for sale anywhere else.

What to look for when buying books

You know exactly what book you're looking for. You know where to go, and you search, and a dozen results pop up. Now what? How do you sort through them? What do you look for on the listing?

Copyright Page

The first thing to check is if there's a picture of the copyright page. That will, the overwhelming majority of the time, tell you exactly what printing the book is. If there's not a picture of the copyright page, you can try to figure out if it's a first state based on other pictures, such as the price on the dust jacket. However, I always recommend messaging the seller and asking for a picture of the copyright page if there's even the slightest doubt on which printing it is.

Condition

Not all 1/1 copies of a book are worth the same amount. Damages or issues to look for include:

Tears of any sort, especially on the dust jacket. Taped up tears count, and will still significantly impact the value. A missing dust jacket can be a big detractor as well. However, in some cases, it's not too expensive to get another copy of the book and take the dust jacket for the original copy. This works out particularly well if the copy missing the dust jacket is signed, or if you can pull a dust jacket from a second printing because it's identical.

Pages being bent or torn will also majorly devalue a book. Small stains on the page block aren't usually as big of a deal, but a remainder mark also negatively impacts value. In some cases these can be sanded off, but that's not something to count on being able to do, unless you're a professional book restoration expert.

Stamps or writing (other than a signature or line by Sanderson) are also a big downside on books. Ex-library books are rarely collected, unless there's no other way to get them.

Note that damage to the book is different from a misprint. Misprints are cool and, to the right collector (hi, that would be me), worth something.

As with the copyright page, if there are no pictures of the condition of a book, please message the seller and ask. If it looks like the pictures cut off in a suspicious place, ask for a full picture. Please. Check with the seller before you buy. It's a waste of your time and their money if you have to return a book.

Prices

Once you have a book that you know is in the condition you want, and it's exactly what you want, you should make sure you're paying the right amount for it. The final main section of this book goes over the prices of all the main collectible books in detail, and attempts to give an estimated price. That price is also only a rough estimation. Prices fluctuate, especially when there's a new release or a big change in the fanbase.

Still, do your best to only buy a book if it's in the right price range or below. Don't overpay just because you want something now. If the book is valued under $1,000, I can almost guarantee that other copies will come up for sale in the next 6-12 months, if not sooner, and collecting is very much a patience game.

You can definitely find deals on used book sales, from sellers who don't quite know what they have. But you are more likely to find someone attempting to scam you, listing something as a "first edition" when it's a 23rd printing, hoping you'll not notice and think you're getting a deal on the price. Be careful of this, and if you're ever in doubt, ask some of the administration in the SCG about the book. We will not snipe the listing from you, and will do our best to verify that the pictures are what the listing says. It benefits nobody in the collecting community when someone gets scammed, so we actively try to prevent it.

Known sellers

While it's never a sure thing, known sellers, both in the guild and on eBay/Mercari/AbeBooks, will be more reliable than a new person with no reviews or ratings. You should always check a seller's feedback and ratings. Known sellers, even small personal ones, should have at least a few tens of ratings, if not hundreds. In the guild, you can ask for references.

On the other end of the spectrum, be wary of some of the high volume sellers. They sell too many books to care about individual listings, and will reuse pictures or slap on copy/pasted descriptions without ever looking at the actual book they are selling. BetterWorldBooks is notorious for this and for not shipping their books well, so I will never buy from them again.

Refund policy

One thing to check with sellers, especially on eBay, is the return policy they have. Many will have a blanket return policy to allow you to return anything you don't like, and Mercari enforces this on all of their sellers, but not all sellers across other platforms will have this same policy. If you're making a risky purchase, check the return policy first.

Where and how to sell books

On the flip side from buying books, some collectors want to sell their books too. If you've been around for a while, or you grabbed something nice at a garage sale and would much rather have a good reading copy that you don't have to worry about damaging, you might want to sell your books.

Websites to use

Mercari is not a good place to sell books anymore. They have very buyer-centric policies, and will give a refund for pretty much everything, and I have heard of numerous cases of buyers abusing this policy to scam sellers. They also charge fees blatantly to the buyers, which has made a lot of people unhappy.

I have never known anyone who has sold anything on AbeBooks, so I don't know much about their policies. They are good for listing books with lots of details. Buyers there will know exactly what they're looking for, and there's no auctions or haggling for prices.

If you have a rare book and you want a wide audience for it, eBay is your best bet for running an auction, but be sure to review the fees. At the time of printing, eBay collects 14.95% of the final sale price of books.

If you want to sell straight to another collector, go with the Sanderson Collectors Guild Discord server. You will still pay a small fee with using Goods and Services (currently 2.99%) to get protection from PayPal, but it's still the lowest fee you'll see. You will get called out, however, if you price something incorrectly.

What to include in your listing

Wherever you list, if you're listing a collectible book, include as much detail as you can. If it's a first printing, say that it is. And include a picture of the copyright page and any other pictures you need to prove that it is. Post pictures of the text block to show if there is a remainder mark or not. Make it clear exactly what condition your book is in. If the book is signed, show that off! If there's a personalization, make sure to include that too - it's a lie by omission if you don't.

Include the ISBN. Always. And mark what edition a book is. If it's a hardcover, explicitly say that. Same if it's a leatherbound.

Put a price in. If you're posting in the Discord and you're open to negotiations, say so, but it's always a good idea to have a starting price so that people know what range you're thinking about. If you're posting an auction on eBay, set the initial price at an amount that you'll actually accept. Don't mess with a reserve price and pretend by setting the initial bid low. Just state what you will accept as a minimum, and let people bid over that if they want it more.

How to price your books

The big section in this book aims to be a general guide on where to price things. Make sure to take into account signatures, damage, etc., as these will modify the base price. In addition, the guild provides the "blue book", a big listing of estimated prices, mainly compiled by Lauren, who does awesome work. I always recommend checking those values, and unlike this printed book, they are updated regularly.

In addition, search for sold listings. On eBay, there is a mildly hidden setting to show all the sold listings, and these can give you a good idea of prices, especially on auctions.

Price your books fairly. Don't try to overprice your books in hopes that someone will not know that the same book can be cheaper. That's not in the spirit of the collecting community, and if other collectors find out that you are doing this, you will become disliked and shunned in the community.

How to ship your books

Carefully.

But seriously. When you're shipping a book, it's something that the recipient has seen. They know what they're getting, and they want it to show up looking like that. They don't want any new damage on the book. And the postal system can be brutal sometimes.

Always use a box. Always. Padded envelopes are not enough. They can get bent and twisted and squished into places. A box is so much more secure.

Pad out your boxes too. A box with a bunch of air space is bad for two reasons. First, the box can easily get crushed in that direction, because there's nothing supporting the edges. Second, it means the book has room to shift. And if the book has room to shift, it can bounce and tear the cover, dent the boards, or bend pages, etc.

Wrap every book as well. Don't just toss them in the padding. Put a tight wrap on each book, even if it's just brown paper. This prevents the book from creasing or bending if there's even the slightest amount of shifting in the contents of the box. And with how much these boxes are tossed around in the hundreds or thousands of miles it will take to reach its destination, moving around will happen.

If possible, use bubble wrap, book crosses, or paper honeycomb wrap. All of these solutions hold the book tight and prevent creasing, but also give an additional layer of padding. If something small pokes through the edge of your box, the book will still be okay. If things shift and one of your books rams into another in the box, the padding will protect both of them. If you include a pin with the book, and despite your best efforts, the box gets crushed and the pin back smashed into the book, the book will be protected.

Insurance is nice, but only really necessary on books over $100 in value. A lot of the time, for small to moderate trades, I will ship my books via USPS media mail. There's no real difference in how carefully a box is handled between the different shipping rates, and media mail is the most cost efficient (though it only allows books), leaving you more of your shipping budget for the protective packaging on the book itself.

Protecting books

You figured out what you want, you found it online, you bought it, the seller shipped it safely to you. Awesome! Now how do you protect your book and keep it looking as good as new? There's a handful of good rules to follow, and I'll do my best to explain them here.

Sunlight is murder

Direct sunlight is the worst thing possible for a book, outside of actively harming the book by dropping it in water or tearing the page or something. It will fade the cover, and it will yellow the pages and make them brittle. It will wear out the book quickly. If at all possible, store your collectible books out of direct sunlight. They can go there for brief moments if you want to take a nice picture, but they cannot stay there.

Mylar dust jacket protectors

The safest thing for your books is to keep them on the shelf and never touch them, but that's not very practical. The entire reason for having a book collection is to have something to admire and enjoy, and you can't enjoy a book very well if you only ever see the spine from a distance.

The dust jacket is generally the most easily damaged part of a book, and so it's the most important part to protect. Mylar dust jacket protectors are very common, very safe to use, and greatly prolong the life of the dust jacket.

These can be bought from many sources online, and there are plenty of tutorials on the internet on how to apply them to your books. The "name brand" among collectors is Brodart, but anything that is archival quality, with acid free backing paper and clear mylar protection, will work for your books.

I recommend watching a video online about how to apply the protectors before you do it, and practicing on a few lower-stakes books before you apply them to your prize possessions.

I personally do not put dust jacket protectors on many of my books, but this is because I take a lot of pictures of my books from all kinds of angles for social media, and the mylar protectors are shiny and cause reflections. Many people like this shine on their books when they look at them, but it does play havoc with pictures. Additionally, I put many reference images on collectingsanderson.com and share informational content on my YouTube channel, and I want the books to look as close to the original as possible.

Removing books from plastic wrap

Plastic wrap is bad for books. It can trap moisture and cause mold on your books. It's great for an initial protective layer when the book is coming from the factory, but as soon as you get a book that is shrink-wrapped in plastic, remove that layer.

This is the same recommendation that Dragonsteel Books gives on their official website about all of their editions. If you don't listen to me, at least listen to them.

Storing books and book shoes

Books should generally be stored upright, in the traditional way on the shelf.

The biggest issue you will run into with storing books in this manner is page block sag. This happens when the book is particularly thick, and the middle pages of the book will pull down and forward, creating a dip. This is particularly prevalent in the *Stormlight* books because of the width of the page block, especially on the original printings of *The Way of Kings* and *Words of Radiance* before they switched to thinner paper. I have also seen it often with the earlier printings of the Mistborn Era One leatherbounds.

Page sag is not an inevitable part of a book's lifespan, however. There are two possible solutions to this. The first is to get a book shoe. These are little bits of archival foam that sit just below the page block on the shelf. They need to be cut to size specifically for the width of the book you're storing. They sit on the shelf, and support the page block from underneath, meaning that they don't pull on the spine of the book and cause the sagging. Typically the desired thickness of these foam boards is 3 to 5 mm, but varies depending on who you get it from. In some cases, book shoes can actually reverse page sag, and they are the preferred solution in the collector community.

The other solution is to store your books laying down. This does work, although it won't correct a sag that has already happened. The issue you run into here is that laying a book down flat and then stacking other books on top of it will apply pressure directly to the spine, from the weight of the other books on top of it, and this can crush the spine and cause it to bow outwards. If you are careful with stacking your books, especially if you alternate the direction of the spine, this can be avoided, but it is still something to keep an eye out for.

Handling books

Wash your hands before handling your rare books.

Hand oils are generally not too bad for a book's pages, unless you handle a book frequently, have very greasy hands, or the book is going to be handled by a bunch of people, but they can still damage a book over time, and it is best policy to have your hands as clean as possible before touching your books.

The easy way to prevent any hand oil damage to a book is to use gloves. I generally recommend white fabric gloves. This recommendation comes from my experience as a quilter, where these gloves are ubiquitous for protecting delicate fabrics. These gloves are fairly inexpensive, and you can keep several pairs on hand and wash them as needed in order to protect your books.

Some collectors do not recommend or like these gloves, however, as they make it easier to catch your hand on a page and bend it. The choice is yours.

When handling a book, be careful not to open the spine too far, as this can cause it to crack and break, especially on paperbacks and glued books.

Humidity and temperature

Books don't react well to extremes of humidity or temperature. If you freeze a book, you're in for a bad time. If you soak a book with water, you're in for an absolutely horrible time. In general, keep books inside, in a climate controlled environment. In general, this is most important when putting books in a storage unit, as most houses will already be a pretty good environment. If they get too hot for too long, the pages will get brittle. If they get too humid, the pages will start to get wavy and uneven.

Cataloging books

There are many services out there for listing the books that you've read, but none of the popular ones have a system to record which edition of the book you have, nor have a way to list condition, how many copies you have, if the book is signed, etc.

At least in the Sanderson collecting community, there is a solution: collectingsanderson.com. This is a web site put together by a collector and fan, Jimmy Conner. He coded the whole website himself, pulling in data from a database that Austin, Luke, and I had compiled of many of our editions. It has all the features listed above, as well as high resolution pictures of the actual editions that you're looking at on each book.

It's not fully comprehensive on all of the editions, but you're always welcome to submit feedback to the admins (I'm the main one who looks at it) about the data that is missing.

The website itself is fairly straightforward, although it can take a little getting used to. I posted a video on my YouTube channel a while back about how to use it, titled "Collecting Sanderson Dot Com is now Live", and I recommend watching that for an introduction. There is an entire channel in the SCG Discord about the website, and Jimmy and myself will be happy to answer your questions if you post in there.

There is a project underway to rewrite the website in another programming language to make it more extensible and allow more of us to code on it, but that's not going to be a quick process, and is currently on hold as several of us in that group recently switched jobs, or have been beta reading or writing, etc.

If having your book collection in someone else's database isn't for you, or you don't want to go through the process of inputting all the data one book at a time, it's perfectly fine to keep a spreadsheet listing everything. I did this for many years, and I know several other very avid collectors who still do. If you do this, I recommend at least listing the book title, printing, edition/state, and ISBN. For finance reasons, I also very much like to track the amount spent on each book, but that's more up to personal preference.

Signed Sanderson Books

One of the most collectible parts of many books is the signature. Sanderson is an absolute signing machine, and can be seen regularly on Intentionally Blank (the podcast that he runs where he chats with Dan Wells for a little under an hour each week about completely random stuff) signing tip-in pages. At pretty much every convention he attends, there are lines to get his signature, and fans will pay a premium to get a book that has been signed by Sanderson. It's important to recognize Sanderson's signature, and be able to make sure your book is legitimately signed.

Identifying Sanderson's signature

These days, Sanderson's signature is very standardized, because he has signed tens if not hundreds of thousands of books with it. Sanderson's signature is quick and flowing, and designed to be done only with elbow and shoulder movements. Sanderson designed it this way so that even on massive signing days, he would not hurt his wrist. It should look effortless.

It looks like this:

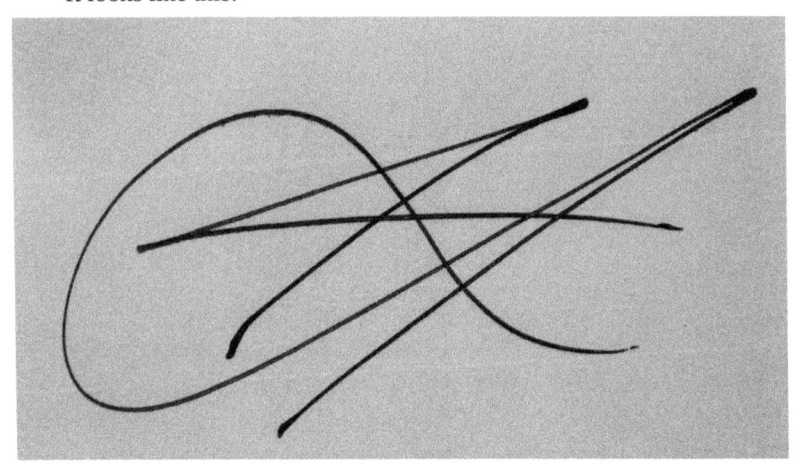

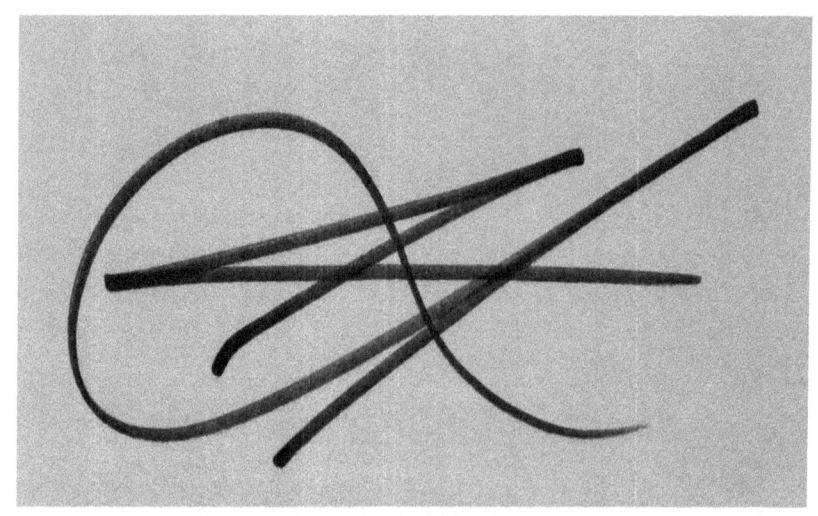

However, it has not always looked like that. On occasion you will find early books (*Elantris, Mistborn, Alcatraz 1*) signed with earlier versions of Sanderson's signature. Here is an example of that early signature, from my ABM of *Mistborn*:

I have a special sheet of paper, given to me by Kara who runs the Dragonsteel store, that shows some of Sanderson's signature progression over time. Sanderson signed this sheet for players playing Magic with him at one of his conventions, to illustrate how his signature changed over time. It's really fun because in the earliest versions you can distinctly see the "B" and "S" for his name, and see how they morphed into the quick version he does today.

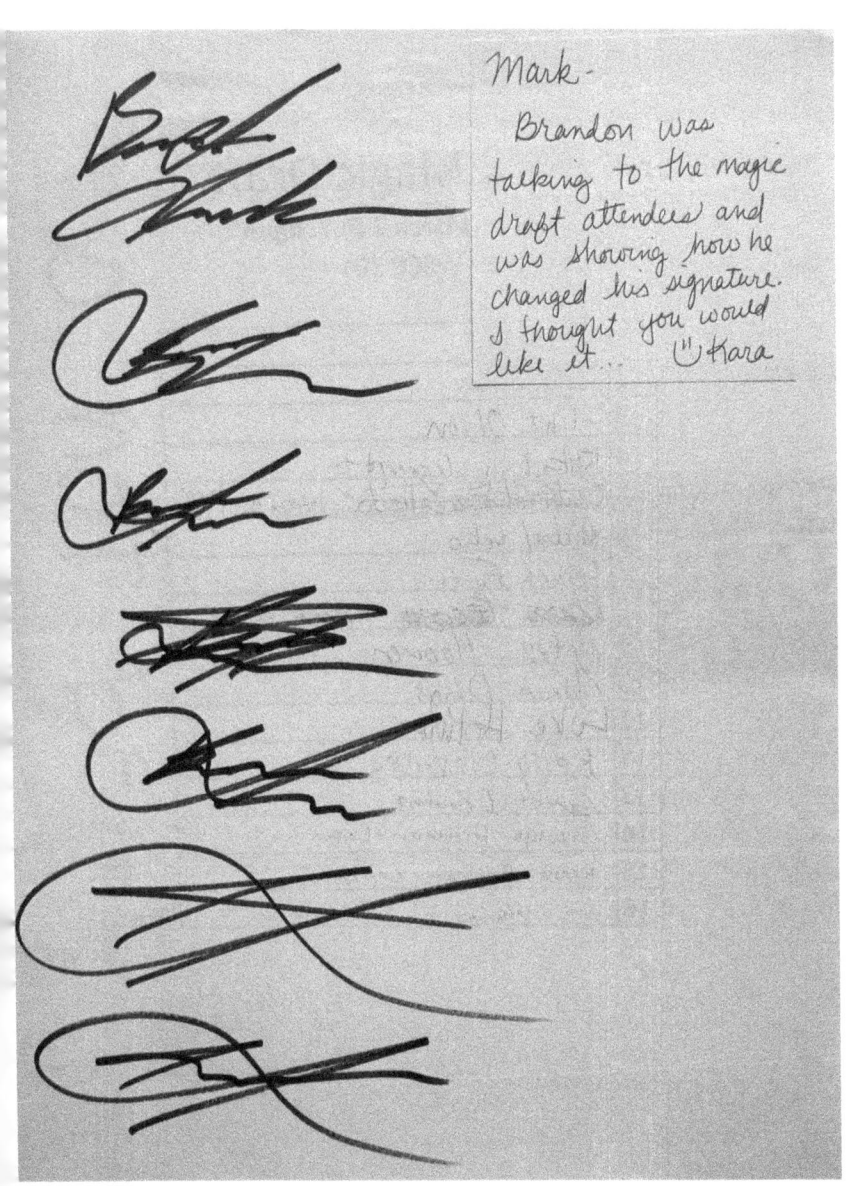

> Mark –
>
> Brandon was talking to the magic draft attendees and was showing how he changed his signature. I thought you would like it... ☺ Kara

Getting a signed book

In ye olden days, before the pandemic, Sanderson did two things differently: He used to offer most of his hardcovers signed in the webstore, including all of the leatherbounds signed, and he toured to dozens of conventions and bookstores every year, signing books for pretty much anyone who

41

showed up at any of them. Signing lines were not limited to first come first serve or a lottery, and lines often ran 5+ hours.

These days, the store does not stock many signed books outside of new releases, and even the leatherbounds are not always signed. This is because demand for the books got too high for Sanderson to sign enough copies without significantly impacting his writing time, so now he has a few dedicated hours of signing every few weeks, and it's almost always for trying to catch up with the leatherbounds.

Sanderson also does not tour for any book releases anymore, maybe does one release day event, and only goes to two or three conventions per year. At these conventions, you have to get a ticket specifically for his signing. Tickets either run out in only a few minutes, or are luck-based. Even at his own convention, Dragonsteel Nexus, where Sanderson is the main attraction for 3 days, there is only about a 50% chance (this year, 2024) that you will get a ticket to get anything signed by him after buying a ticket to the convention.

Most of the signing opportunities these days are for lightning signings. In a lightning signing, you stand there with your singular book open, and Sanderson walks down the line and signs the books. One signature, and there is no time for personalization, chatting with him, or for posed photos, so be sure to have someone ready to snap a candid photo for you.

If you are very lucky, you can get a traditional signing line ticket. This ticket will get you three books with a quick signature, as well as one book personalized, which can include a quote from the book.

Value of a signed book

A signature tends to add $75-$100 to the value of pretty much any book now. This includes books that are signed (and numbered) upon release. In pretty much every release that I can remember recently, excluding *Bastille*, signed copies have sold out before the book was actually released, and less than a year later the signed copies commanded a premium.

Books that did not have a signed release run, such as the secret projects, cost even more for signed copies. Often these prices can run $300 extra for a signed copy. Be prepared to pay if you want one, and if you have an opportunity to attend a con and get four books signed in a traditional signing line with Sanderson, I highly recommend prioritizing these books.

Other things can affect the value of a signed book as well. A personalized signed book is worth maybe half of what a plain signed book is. A lined and/or dated book can be worth slightly more, and a numbered copy can be worth significantly more, depending on the number and how many books were numbered. For recent releases where upwards of 5,000 numbered books were available, the numbered copies are far more common than plain signed copies, and add maybe $50 to the value unless it's a really low number, like below 100. For very old books where Sanderson only numbered a few copies on release, or the secret projects where he only numbered 50 copies of each, a number commands a massive premium. Numbered secret projects are worth five to ten times the value of a signed copy.

Bookplates

Bookplates are little stickers that are signed. You can take a bookplate and put it in any book you want, and some people will consider that book signed. Sanderson's bookplates used to be sold for $5 for a pack of 5 on his website, but that is no longer the case, and they have become rare.

Signed Sanderson bookplates can run upwards of $50 these days, but often don't add even that much to the value of a book. Many collectors would rather have an unsigned book with the chance to get Sanderson to sign their book directly some day.

The true value in bookplates comes after an author has passed away. Robert Jordan bookplates, for example, often run upwards of $200-250.

There have been a couple of special releases that have had their own bookplates, which are cool and collectible. For example, the *White Sand Omnibus* "signed" deluxe edition from Dynamite was actually just a custom bookplate. The first 500 preorders of *Dark One* from Dragonsteel also came with a custom bookplate.

Facsimile signatures: The Wheel of Time

You will see listings for the last three *Wheel of Time* books, the ones that Sanderson co-wrote, on eBay claiming they are signed at least once a week. These listings are rarely correct. Because Sanderson felt uncomfortable signing any *Wheel of Time* books that did not have Robert Jordan's signature in them, he asked Tor to print a scan of Jordan's signature into the books. Tor did so, and I have seen this signature across every edition in every language I have looked at.

Needless to say, a printed signature does not make a book signed. True signed copies of those last 3 books are ones that have Sanderson's signature, and it is frustrating to sort through the noise online to find one of these.

Thankfully these are the only books that have a printed signature on the title page. Some of the Tor/Gollancz editions of the secret projects have

Sanderson's signature printed on the back of the book, but we have not seen these being sold as "signed" so far.

Sanderson-adjacent signatures

Sanderson-adjacent signatures come in two varieties: There are people who collaborated or worked on something directly with Sanderson. Art for his books, a story co-written with him, etc. And there are people who happen to show up with him very often in anthologies. The most popular of both categories are listed below, with pictures.

Isaac Stewart

Isaac is the art director at Dragonsteel, the creator of the *Mistborn* Steel Alphabet and the *Stormlight* glyphs, and the cartographer for many of the maps in Sanderson's books. His name in the acknowledgments typically has a funky symbol replacing one of the letters.

Michael Whelan

Whelan is the cover artist for the first five *Stormlight* books, and the most famous artist to have done covers or art for Sanderson.

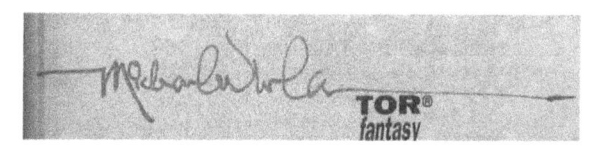

Ben McSweeney

Ben McSweeney is an artist who has done many things, the most popular of which are the Mistborn Era Two broadsheets and Shallan's sketchbook pages in the *Stormlight* books.

Ben McSweeney
Symbols & Cartography

Peter Ahlstrom

Peter is Sanderson's right-hand man. He is the head of Sanderson's in-house editorial team. His name in the acknowledgments typically has an "in-" adjective in front of it.

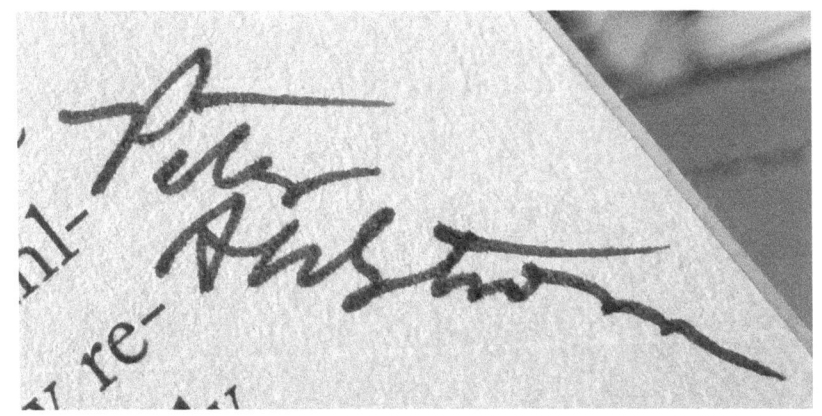

Janci Patterson

Janci is the co-writer for *Bastille vs. The Evil Librarians* and the *Skyward Flight* novellas plus *Hyperthief*. She is currently cowriting the sequel series to *Skyward* as well. Her signature can vary a bit, so I have included two examples.

Hayley Lazo

Hayley is the artist for all of the *Alcatraz* sketches in the Starscape editions, as well as many of the *Skyward* illustrations of taynix, and the corresponding card deck.

Howard Lyon

Howard is a Magic: the Gathering artist who has also done a lot of art for Sanderson's books. Many of the illustrations in the leatherbound are his, as well as the endpapers for Oathbringer. He also did the Marewill flower art on the US cover of *Mistborn: Secret History,* and illustrated the Dragonsteel edition of *Tress.*

Steve Argyle

Steve is also a Magic artist, known for cards like Bloodbraid Elf and Liliana of the Veil. In Sanderson's works, he illustrated *The Frugal Wizard's Handbook for Surviving Medieval England*, and provided many illustrations for the leatherbounds, including the full Knights Radiant order woodcut illustrations in *The Way of Kings* and endpapers for *Mistborn*.

Miranda Meeks

Miranda has done a handful of pieces of official art, including the cover for the US hardcover release of *Legion: The Many Lives of Stephen Leeds*, the cover of the Shadows part of the *Shadows for Silence in the Forests of Hell/Perfect State* con double, and various pieces of leatherbound artwork.

Dan Dos Santos

Dan Dos Santos did the cover art for the US edition of *Warbreaker*, as well as multiple art pieces from that book's leatherbound. He also did some of the *Stormlight* Herald endpapers, and the fashion folio art pages.

Dan Wells

Dan Wells is a writer. He first appeared in the *Altered Perceptions* anthology with Sanderson, and later *Shadows Beneath*. He wrote the foreword to the tenth anniversary editions of *Elantris*. He is currently writing many of the game books and other materials for the Cosmere RPG made by Brotherwise Games. He was also one of the founding members of the Writing Excuses podcast. He is employed full time by Dragonsteel, is planning to write his own Cosmere novel set on his own world, wrote *Dark One: Forgotten*, and appears with Brandon on Intentionally Blank almost every week.

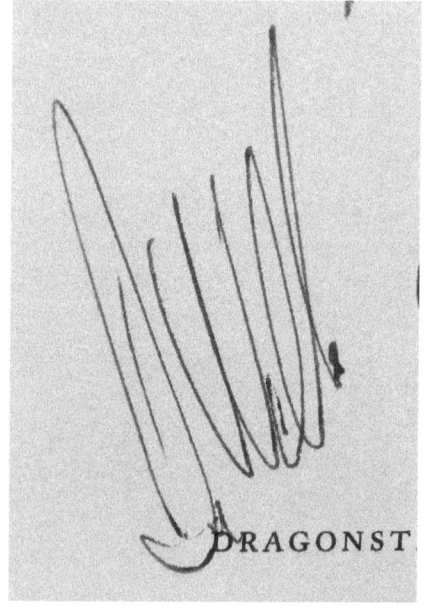

Howard Tayler

Howard is a writer and a cartoonist. In addition to being one of the founding members of the Writing Excuses podcast, he appeared in *Altered Perceptions* and *Shadows Beneath* with Sanderson.

Mary Robinette Kowal

Mary Robinette is a writer and audiobook narrator. She co-wrote *The Original* with Sanderson, though no physical copies have been published. In addition, she was on Writing Excuses for many years, and is in the *Altered Perceptions* and *Shadows Beneath* anthologies with Sanderson.

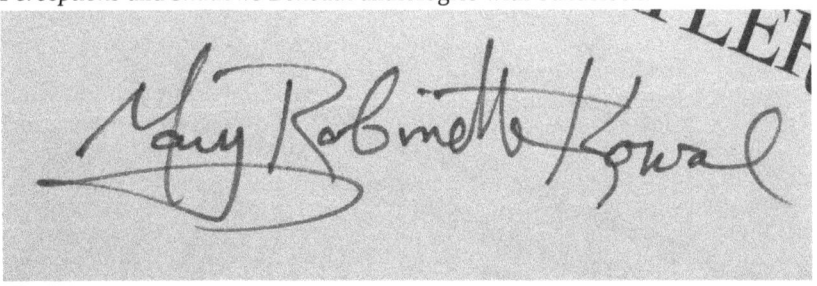

Kazu Kibuishi

Kazu is the illustrator for *The Most Boring Book Ever*.

UISHI

ew York

Collectible Books

This concludes the section on general collecting terminology and tips. The remainder of this book is a listing of all of the editions of Sanderson's works that I consider collectible. I have included every US and UK hardcover release, as well as all of the leatherbounds, the few rare paperbacks, every ARC that I know of, and any other books I think a general Sanderson collector would want. They are organized in two sections: Cosmere and Non-Cosmere. Each section is broken down by series, and ordered approximately by the release date of the first book in that series, though I'm sure there are some deviations.

Each entry has the ISBN, release year, publisher, cover price, and cover artist for that edition. I have also included my best guess at a fair sale value for each book. For most of the books, I also include a few sentences of notes about what makes the book collectible or influences the price, or any traps you need to be aware of when searching for a copy. Unless otherwise stated, all entries are specifically talking about the first printing of that edition.

While you can read the section straight through for a thorough understanding of all the collectible editions, and to help you figure out which editions you may be missing, it is also meant to be a reference guide that you can look at when trying to check a specific book or edition.

Collectible Books - The Cosmere

The Cosmere is Sanderson's mega-universe of connected worlds that share a common set of magical principles and have overlap between the characters. It is, by far, his most popular universe, and comparisons are often made to the Marvel Cinematic Universe. Sanderson tends to keep tight control over the Cosmere, not letting anyone outside write in the universe, though he may lighten those restrictions in the future, as Dan Wells is writing for the RPG and will have his own Cosmere book at some point, and Isaac Stewart has written a *Mistborn* novel.

Elantris

I didn't quite know what to call this series. Right now, it consists of two very loosely related books, *Elantris* and *The Emperor's Soul*, both set on the planet of Sel.

Elantris

Sanderson's first published book. There are four collectible editions.

ABM

There is an Advance Bound Manuscript for this book. The only copy I have ever seen resides in the collection of Sanderson himself. It has a yellow cover with no cover art, and is slightly smaller than the finished hardcover. If you have a lead on a copy, please tell me!

ARC

ISBN	9780765311771
Release Year	2005
Publisher	Tor Books
Cover Price	N/A
Cover Artist	Stephan Martinière
Estimated Value	$1500+

Trade Paperback size, softcover, with the final cover art.

The Advance Reader's Copy of Elantris is much more common than the ABM, though it is still a very rare and highly collectible Cosmere ARC.

Hardcover

| ISBN | 9780765311771 |

Release Year	2005
Publisher	Tor Books
Cover Price	24.95 USD / 34.95 CAN
Cover Artist	Stephan Martinière
Estimated Value	$300+

Elantris is the earliest of the Sanderson collectibles. However, it is not part of his major series (*Mistborn, Stormlight*), so the value is slightly lower than you might expect. The hardcover has a relatively low first print run, as it was his debut novel. Make sure you're getting the original hardcover and not the 10th anniversary edition with ISBN 9780765383105.

Leatherbound 1st Edition

ISBN	9780765388070
Release Year	2015
Publisher	Dragonsteel
Cover Price	100 USD
Cover Artist	Isaac Stewart
Estimated Value	$800+ (numbered)

The first leatherbound edition that Dragonsteel released. There are some formatting issues that they improved with the second edition of the leatherbound, ISBN 9781938570193, released March 2020. In the second edition, they reflowed the text so that each chapter starts on its own page, and this made the book thicker. Additionally, the spine was reformatted. If the circle around the Dragonsteel logo on the spine goes outside the decorative background, it's first edition, otherwise it's second edition. The collectible (numbered) version is the 1/1, not the 2/1. However, if you want the one that looks best on your shelf, the second edition is nicer.

The Emperor's Soul

An absolutely delightful novella set on the same world as *Elantris*. There are three collectible editions in the US, one in the UK, and one from Bulgaria. In addition, this story was reprinted in *Arcanum Unbounded*. See that section for more info.

ARC

ISBN	9781616960926
Release Year	2012
Publisher	Tachyon

Cover Price	N/A
Cover Artist	Alexander Nanitchkov
Estimated Value	$800+

Other than the standard ARC signage about not being for sale and including promo info, this is nearly identical to the paperback edition. Same size, same cover art, etc.

Paperback

ISBN	9781616960926
Release Year	2012
Publisher	Tachyon
Cover Price	14.95 USD
Cover Artist	Alexander Nanitchkov
Estimated Value	$50

One of the few collectible Sanderson paperbacks. The paperback of The Emperor's Soul was the first actual release of this book, coming well before the hardcover. Thus, collectors of true firsts hunt this one down. Despite this, it had a decently large print run and is not hugely expensive. When hunting a 1st print, careful not to get confused with the 10th anniversary paperback, ISBN 9781616964023, cover price $16.95, released in 2022.

Numbered copies of this book are the paperback and not the hardcover, making it the only numbered paperback release I can think of.

Later printings of the paperback have a "HUGO AWARD WINNER" emblem on the front.

Hardcover

ISBN	9781616961510
Release Year	2012
Publisher	Tachyon
Cover Price	25 USD
Cover Artist	Alexander Nanitchkov
Estimated Value	$150

Limited to a print run of 1,000 for the first hardcover printing. The cover is NOT embossed, unlike later printings. The copyright page lacks a number line, but explicitly states "This hardcover edition limited to 1,000 copies". It does not have any signage about winning the Hugo Award.

While released after the paperback, this hardcover was limited and is still highly collectible. Many collectors prefer it over the paperback, just to have the maximum number of books in their collection be hardcovers.

UK Legion and The Emperor's Soul Hardcover

ISBN	9780575116177
Release Year	2013
Publisher	Gollancz
Cover Price	18.99 GBP
Cover Artist	Sam Green
Estimated Value	$100

An interesting bindup, mixing a Cosmere and non-Cosmere novella. This was one of the first UK hardcover editions of Sanderson's, and thus had a relatively low print run and is collectible. I have never seen a hardcover of a later than 1st printing, but that doesn't mean they don't exist.

Fun fact: This book is the one I collected in my first ever YouTube video!

Bulgarian Hardcover

ISBN	9786191930791
Release Year	2017
Publisher	Artline Studios
Cover Price	14.99 BGN
Cover Artist	N/A
Estimated Value	$50

Calling this book a hardcover is doing it a disservice. The front and back boards are made of painted wood, making this one of the coolest and most unique editions of a book in any translation. Each book is unique and distinctive, due to the grain patterns in the wood it was painted on. Out of print, and the price is rising.

The Hope of Elantris

A short story set during the events of *Elantris*. It is available for free to read on Sanderson's website, and has a very cute backstory to go with it. The only printings of this story are in *Arcanum Unbounded*. See that book for more info.

Mistborn

One of Sanderson's two main series, the other being *Stormlight*. *Mistborn* has one of the coolest concepts in fiction, as we watch a world over centuries, stopping to look in on society at different stages of technology and advancement. Books in this series are highly collectible, due to the popularity of the series.

Era 1

The original trilogy. These books were the ones Sanderson wrote that got him picked to finish *The Wheel of Time*. Sanderson often calls them his "calling card", a digestible epic fantasy series that has a satisfying conclusion in its own right, but is still meaty and, well, epic.

Mistborn

There are six collectible editions of this book, though I have included a seventh because I love that edition.

ABM

ISBN	9780765311788
Release Year	2006
Publisher	Tor Books
Cover Price	N/A
Cover Artist	N/A
Estimated Value	$2000+

As with all Advance Bound Manuscripts, this one is very valuable and highly collectible. Copies can be found with Sanderson's early signature in them. It is a blue book with no cover art, slightly shorter than the ARC and hardcover.

ARC

ISBN	9780765311788
Release Year	2006
Publisher	Tor Books
Cover Price	N/A
Cover Artist	N/A
Estimated Value	$1000+

As the first book in one of Sanderson's most iconic series, this is a highly collectible ARC, and copies regularly sell for high prices. It is white, and does not have the cover art, but is trade paperback sized and has the page formatting to match the hardcover.

Hardcover

ISBN	9780765311788

Release Year	2006
Publisher	Tor Books
Cover Price	27.95 USD / 37.95 CAN
Cover Artist	Jon Foster
Estimated Value	$200+

This was before Sanderson was popular, and has a relatively low print run, yet is one of his most popular series, making this a prized collectible to find.

Leatherbound

ISBN	9781938570131
Release Year	2016
Publisher	Dragonsteel
Cover Price	100 USD
Cover Artist	Isaac Stewart
Estimated Value	$500 ($700+ if numbered)

The second of the leatherbound books released by Dragonsteel. They definitely learned some lessons from *Elantris*, and the page formatting and flow is much better here. In addition, instead of just pulling in alternate cover art, this book includes a few pieces of artwork commissioned specifically for it. The first printing of the leatherbound does not quite match the first printings of the other two in the series, as Dragonsteel adjusted the height as they went.

In addition, sometime around the sixth printing, the leather that they were using for this edition stopped being produced. It was named "Corona", and the printing company didn't like the association with the coronavirus, and thus discontinued it. The replacement leather is very similar in color, but there is a noticeable difference if you put the books side by side.

Grim Reaper Mass Market Paperback

ISBN	9780765350381
Release Year	2007
Publisher	Tor Books
Cover Price	7.99 USD / 10.99 CAN
Cover Artist	Jon Foster
Estimated Value	$25

The cover that infamously almost killed Sanderson's career. For reasons that nobody quite understands, when Tor put this book out as a mass market paperback, they commissioned a new cover by the same artist as the hardcover, but much, much worse.

We aren't even sure who the main character is on the cover. For years, I thought it was Kelsier, but I know many others just as convinced it's Vin. We all assume that the "grim reaper" in the background is meant to be some kind of Steel Inquisitor.

This book exists in both first and second printings. It is the only case I can think of where the printing doesn't matter, as collectors want this one just for the horrible cover art. The estimated price is for either printing. By the third printing, Tor wised up and changed to the Chris McGrath cover art of Vin, which is not collectible.

UK 10th Anniversary Hardcover - The Final Empire

ISBN	9781473216815
Release Year	2016
Publisher	Gollancz
Cover Price	14.99 GBP
Cover Artist	us-now.com
Estimated Value	$30 ($100 numbered)

This pocket-sized casewrapped edition is the only UK hardcover of *Mistborn*. The initial release was, like *Elantris* and *Warbreaker*, just a paperback, and Gollancz never went back and did a full hardcover treatment.

This is also the only case where the title of a book has changed significantly in the UK versus the US, here taking on the title *The Final Empire*, which is only a subtitle in the US edition, and not found on the cover of the book.

Anderida Books did a limited run of 200 signed, numbered, tip-in copies. They do not have a separate ISBN.

Yes, the cover artist is a website. That's what the credits in the book say.

Spanish Illustrated Hardcover

ISBN	9788418037214
Release Year	2021
Publisher	Nova
Cover Price	N/A
Cover Artist	Isaac Stewart
Estimated Value	$40

Not necessarily a collectible/rare book, this is just one that I think is particularly pretty and deserves note. It is readily available in Spanish (though you may have to pay international shipping), and contains several pieces of artwork commissioned specifically for this volume, much in the style of the leatherbound or deluxe editions from Dragonsteel, but the pieces are completely unique to the Spanish edition.

The Well of Ascension

The second book in the *Mistborn* trilogy. Many people say it is slower-paced than the first, and while I think that viewpoint has merit, the layering of foreshadowing and information here with the complex political maneuvers is masterful upon a reread.

ABM

ISBN	9780765316882
Release Year	2007
Publisher	Tor Books
Cover Price	N/A
Cover Artist	N/A
Estimated Value	$2000+

A red volume, with no cover art and early text, that is the same size as the *Mistborn* ABM, and slightly shorter than the trade paperback size of the ARC.

ARC

ISBN	9780765316882
Release Year	2007
Publisher	Tor Books
Cover Price	N/A
Cover Artist	N/A
Estimated Value	$900+

White cover, but still no cover art. Standard ARC/trade paperback size.

US Hardcover

ISBN	9780765316882
Release Year	2007
Publisher	Tor Books
Cover Price	27.95 USD / 34.95 CAN
Cover Artist	Jon Foster
Estimated Value	$250+

Thanks in part to the Grim Reaper edition's poor sales, and thanks in part to being the second book in a series, Tor wasn't as confident with *The Well of Ascension*, and printed fewer hardcovers than they did for *Mistborn*. This makes the book rarer and more valuable, despite being newer.

Leatherbound

ISBN	9781938570186
Release Year	2017
Publisher	Dragonsteel
Cover Price	100 USD
Cover Artist	Isaac Stewart
Estimated Value	$400 ($700+ if numbered)

The same notes as *Mistborn* leatherbound apply here: some later printings have a different leather and will match the others in the trilogy in height. The 1/1 does not match.

UK 10th Anniversary Hardcover

ISBN	9781473223080
Release Year	2017
Publisher	Gollancz
Cover Price	16.99 GBP
Cover Artist	us-now.com
Estimated Value	$30 ($100 numbered)

Same notes as the *Mistborn* UK 10th Anniversary Hardcover, including 200 numbered Anderida books copies.

Spanish Illustrated Hardcover

ISBN	9788418037276
Release Year	2021
Publisher	Nova
Cover Price	29.90 Euro
Cover Artist	Isaac Stewart
Estimated Value	$40

Same notes as the *Mistborn* Spanish Illustrated Hardcover.

The Hero of Ages

The climax of the Mistborn Era One series, and still one of the best and most satisfying books ever written. Sanderson pulls out all the stops on emotions with this one, and it's the book that seals the *Mistborn* series as one of many people's favorites.

ARC

ISBN	9780765316899
Release Year	2008
Publisher	Tor Books
Cover Price	N/A
Cover Artist	Jon Foster
Estimated Value	$500+

The only Era One book that has the cover art on the ARC. Trade paperback size.

US Hardcover

ISBN	9780765316899
Release Year	2008
Publisher	Tor Books
Cover Price	27.95 CAN / 30.95 CAN
Cover Artist	Jon Foster
Estimated Value	$75

By this time, the Grim Reaper cover had been replaced, and Sanderson's sales were going back up. Tor had more confidence in him, and a decent number of these were printed. While we do not know exact numbers, it is likely that this is the most common of the Era One hardcovers, and it appropriately holds the lowest value.

Leatherbound

ISBN	9781938570209
Release Year	2018
Publisher	Dragonsteel
Cover Price	100 USD
Cover Artist	Isaac Stewart
Estimated Value	$400 ($700+ if numbered)

The same notes here as the *Mistborn* leatherbound. Later printings have new leather and match the others in height.

UK 10th Anniversary Hardcover

ISBN	9781473223059
Release Year	2018

Publisher	Gollancz
Cover Price	16.99 GBP
Cover Artist	us-now.com
Estimated Value	$30 ($100 if numbered)

Same notes as the *Mistborn* UK 10th Anniversary Hardcover, including numbering limitation of 200.

Spanish Illustrated Hardcover

ISBN	9788418037290
Release Year	2021
Publisher	Nova
Cover Price	N/A
Cover Artist	Isaac Stewart
Estimated Value	$40

Same notes here as for the *Mistborn* Spanish Illustrated Hardcover.

Era 2

The Alloy of Law

The first book of a new era! Featuring a lawman with a grudge against society, his crazy sidekick, and an ex-lawman with some valid points.

ARC

ISBN	9780765330420
Release Year	2011
Publisher	Tor Books
Cover Price	N/A
Cover Artist	Christian McGrath
Estimated Value	$1000+

Trade paperback, standard ARC size, with cover art.

US Hardcover

ISBN	9780765330420
Release Year	2011
Publisher	Tor Books
Cover Price	24.99 USD / 28.99 CAN
Cover Artist	Christian McGrath
Estimated Value	$50

By this point, Sanderson was very popular (post *Wheel of Time* and *The Way of Kings*), so there were a large number of these printed, and they still appear for sale fairly regularly.

Fun Mark fact: This was the first book I bought a 1/1 hardcover of when already having the paperback, making it the first time I bought a book just to collect it.

Leatherbound

ISBN	9781938570285
Release Year	2022
Publisher	Dragonsteel
Cover Price	100 USD
Cover Artist	Isaac Stewart
Estimated Value	$100 ($350+ if numbered)

Released initially as part of a bundle on the Dragonsteel store with *Shadows of Self*. The 1,500 numbered copies sold out in under ten minutes despite issues with the queue on the webstore. Numbers between this and Shadows were *not* matching, and getting a set is quite hard.

UK Hardcover

ISBN	9780575105805
Release Year	2011
Publisher	Gollancz
Cover Price	18.99 GBP
Cover Artist	Sam Green
Estimated Value	$300

In stark contrast to the US hardcover, this was one of the first Sanderson books published in hardcover by Gollancz, and had a comparatively low print run and is quite rare and hard to find. Later printings do exist, but the book is out of print in hardcover, so those are rare and not cheap either.

Spanish Illustrated Hardcover

ISBN	9788419260215
Release Year	2024
Publisher	Nova
Cover Price	N/A
Cover Artist	Isaac Stewart
Estimated Value	$40

Same notes here as for the *Mistborn* Spanish Illustrated Hardcover.

Shadows of Self

Initially planned as the first of a follow-up "trilogy" to *The Alloy of Law*, this book dives deep into political scandals and working class wages, and features another villain with some very valid points.

I do not list a Spanish Illustrated Hardcover for this one yet because that book is not out yet. It will be within the next year, and I will add it to the guide when it is.

ARC

ISBN	9780765378552
Release Year	2015
Publisher	Tor Books
Cover Price	N/A
Cover Artist	Christian McGrath
Estimated Value	$800+

Trade paperback, standard ARC size, with cover art.

US Hardcover

ISBN	9780765378552
Release Year	2015
Publisher	Tor Books
Cover Price	27.99 USD / 32.5 CAN
Cover Artist	Christian McGrath
Estimated Value	$40

Easy to find in used bookstores/online.

Leatherbound

ISBN	9781938570292
Release Year	2022
Publisher	Dragonsteel
Cover Price	100 USD
Cover Artist	Isaac Stewart
Estimated Value	$100 ($350+ if numbered)

See notes for *The Alloy of Law* in leatherbound.

UK Hardcover

ISBN	9781473208216
Release Year	2015

Publisher	Gollancz
Cover Price	18.99 GBP
Cover Artist	Sam Green
Estimated Value	$65 ($200+ if numbered)

The numbered copies are a signed tip-in page by Anderida books, limited to 100.

The Bands of Mourning

This book goes to some cold places. It's also the book where Steris, one of the best characters in all of Sanderson's works, really starts to shine.

Sanderson wrote this book to get over his writing block for *Shadows of Self*. Yes. He literally wrote the entire sequel to get past his writing block. In secret, and then he announced it publicly when it was done. Tor pushed him to release the book only a few months after Shadows of Self, something Sanderson has stated he was not happy with and does not wish to do again.

ARC

ISBN	9780765378576
Release Year	2016
Publisher	Tor Books
Cover Price	N/A
Cover Artist	N/A
Estimated Value	$1000+

Trade paperback, but with no cover art. There were not terribly many of these made, because of the quick release schedule following *Shadows of Self*. Tor figured that people probably wouldn't have read Shadows in time to get and read an ARC of this one and then promote it, is my best guess. It is the rarest of the Era Two ARCs.

US Hardcover

ISBN	9780765378576
Release Year	2016
Publisher	Tor Books
Cover Price	27.99 USD / 32.5 CAN
Cover Artist	Christian McGrath
Estimated Value	$40

Similar notes to the *Shadows of Self* US Hardcover.

UK Hardcover

ISBN	9781473208254
Release Year	2016
Publisher	Gollancz
Cover Price	18.99 GBP
Cover Artist	Sam Green
Estimated Value	$65 ($200+ if numbered)

Similar notes to the *Shadows of Self* UK Hardcover, including Anderida Books limitation of 100.

Leatherbound

ISBN	9781938570476
Release Year	2024
Publisher	Dragonsteel
Cover Price	125 USD
Cover Artist	Sam Green
Estimated Value	$125

Preorders for this book went live October 29, 2024, and books started just in time to get the ISBN. There were 2,000 numbered copies, and despite the "checkout" button being broken on the store for seemingly over half of the fans, numbered copies sold out in about 7 minutes.

The Lost Metal

Supposedly atium. The explosive final volume of the Wax and Wayne series. Sanderson said at the release event that the "gloves are off" with regards to Cosmere references.

ARC

ISBN	9780765391193
Release Year	2022
Publisher	Tor Books
Cover Price	N/A
Cover Artist	Christian McGrath
Estimated Value	$600+

Trade paperback sized, with cover art.

US Hardcover

| ISBN | 9780765391193 |

Release Year	2022
Publisher	Tor Books
Cover Price	29.99 USD / 39.99 CAN
Cover Artist	Christian McGrath
Estimated Value	$30

A recent hardcover with a large first printing, you can still find these for cover price online quite easily.

UK Hardcover

ISBN	9781473215269
Release Year	2022
Publisher	Gollancz
Cover Price	22 GBP
Cover Artist	Sam Green
Estimated Value	$40

I have seen later printings of this one already, so I'm valuing it at slightly over cover price, because I believe (but have no evidence) that the first UK print run was slightly smaller than in the US. There was no Anderida tip-in edition.

Other stories

Mistborn: Secret History

A story that follows a dead man behind the scenes during Mistborn Era One. This story was written on a very tight schedule in secret, and released as an e-book only, on the same day as *The Bands of Mourning*, with the afterword of that book being the only announcement of its release.

This story appears as part of *Arcanum Unbounded*. See that book for more info. The US and UK hardcovers were released after *Arcanum Unbounded*, so if you're just hunting the first physical printing, go for *AU* instead.

US Pocket Hardcover

ISBN	9781250859143
Release Year	2022
Publisher	Tor Books
Cover Price	10.99 USD / 14.99 CAD
Cover Artist	Howard Lyon

| Estimated Value | $15 |

The book has moved on to later printings, so the first printing isn't the default, but it is still very easy to find.

UK Pocket Hardcover

ISBN	9781473225046
Release Year	2019
Publisher	Gollancz
Cover Price	10.99 GBP
Cover Artist	Sam Green
Estimated Value	$25

This one will sometimes show up on eBay with the *Arcanum Unbounded* cover art, also by Sam Green. There is no record of any physical copies existing with that cover image, and I believe those listings are pulling from an e-book cover. Don't buy it thinking you've stumbled on some new edition.

The Eleventh Metal

This story has no standalone editions. You can find it either as part of the *Mistborn Adventure Game*, or in *Arcanum Unbounded*. See the respective books for more info.

Allomancer Jak and the Pits of Eltania

This story originally came from the broadsheets that were included in *The Alloy of Law*. Sanderson later expanded upon it, and it was published in the *Alloy of Law* supplement to the *Mistborn Adventure Game*. It is also included in *Arcanum Unbounded*.

Mistborn Adventure Game and supplements

The base game book contains the first printing of the story *The Eleventh Metal*.

Hardcover

ISBN	9780982684382
Release Year	2012
Publisher	Crafty Games
Cover Price	N/A
Cover Artist	Ben McSweeney
Estimated Value	$100

A limited print run, and out of print well before Crafty lost the license to keep publishing these. There is only one printing. There is no number line, instead it states "First Printing 2012".

Paperback

ISBN	9780982684399
Release Year	2012
Publisher	Crafty Games
Cover Price	N/A
Cover Artist	Ben McSweeney
Estimated Value	$30

This book is still available for sale as of writing from Crafty via Amazon, though their license ended in 2023 and they are not allowed to print new copies. I have not seen a second print. There is no number line, instead it states "First Printing 2012".

Alloy of Law

ISBN	9781940094915
Release Year	2014
Publisher	Crafty Games
Cover Price	34.95 USD
Cover Artist	Ben McSweeney
Estimated Value	$50

This book contains the Allomancer Jak story. There is no number line, instead it states "First Printing 2014".

Terris: Wrought of Copper

ISBN	9781940094908
Release Year	2014
Publisher	Crafty Games
Cover Price	24.95 USD
Cover Artist	Tommy Arnold
Estimated Value	$30

This book contains no Sanderson writing, but as it is Sanderson adjacent and now out-of-print, it is collectible. There is no number line, instead it states "First Printing 2014".

Skaa: Tin and Ash

ISBN	9781940094939

Release Year	2015
Publisher	Crafty Games
Cover Price	24.95 USD
Cover Artist	Tommy Arnold
Estimated Value	$30

This book contains no Sanderson writing, but as it is Sanderson adjacent and now out-of-print, it is collectible. There is no number line, instead it states "First Printing 2015".

Alloy of Law: Masks of the Past

ISBN	9781940094946
Release Year	2017
Publisher	Crafty Games
Cover Price	24.95 USD
Cover Artist	Micah Epstein
Estimated Value	$30

This book contains no Sanderson writing, but as it is Sanderson adjacent and now out-of-print, it is collectible. There is no number line, instead it states "First Printing 2017".

Nobles: The Golden Mandate

ISBN	9781940094953
Release Year	2023
Publisher	Crafty Games
Cover Price	24.95 USD
Cover Artist	Micah Epstein
Estimated Value	$30

This book contains no Sanderson writing, but as it is Sanderson adjacent and now out-of-print, it is collectible. There is no number line, instead it states "First Printing 2023".

Nacidos De La Bruma: Guía de Bolsillo Para la Gran Saga de Fantasía

This book was released in Spain alongside some of the illustrated editions recently. Spanish is Sanderson's best-selling foreign language by a huge margin, and Nova has started to publish as many Sanderson books as they can.

It is a world guide to both eras of *Mistborn*. I believe the book contains some Ben McSweeney art that was commissioned for this edition, and has not been printed anywhere else. It was compiled by Tamara Tonetti and Ángel Lorenzo, who run the Spanish fansite cosmere.es.

Paperback

ISBN	N/A
Release Year	2022
Publisher	Nova
Cover Price	N/A
Cover Artist	Isaac Stewart
Estimated Value	$50

This book has no ISBN, and the cover is the Harmonium symbol by Isaac Stewart. There is no cover price or other info.

There are two states of this book, one with a glossy cover, and one with a matte cover. They are otherwise identical, and due to the lack of printing info, either one is considered a first print and is collectible.

Warbreaker

Sanderson wrote this book after finishing Mistborn Era One, in part as a reaction to the dark and grim world of Scadrial. He (and his publisher) wanted something brighter, and so we get the delightful color-based magic system of Nalthis, and tons of gorgeous art. There are three collectible editions.

As this was early in Sanderson's career, there is no UK hardcover of this book. They have not even come out with an anniversary edition of it.

Warbreaker

ARC

ISBN	9780765320308
Release Year	2009
Publisher	Tor Books
Cover Price	N/A
Cover Artist	Dan Dos Santos
Estimated Value	$600+

Like *Elantris*, not part of a main Cosmere series, so less desired, but still a sought-after ARC.

Hardcover

ISBN	9780765320308
Release Year	2009
Publisher	Tor Books
Cover Price	27.95 USD / 35.95 CAN
Cover Artist	Dan Dos Santos
Estimated Value	$100+

Relatively rare as an earlier Cosmere collectible hardcover. Watch out when buying as the book club edition of this one is very common, and unscrupulous sellers will attempt to get you confused on the two.

The "SciFi Essential Book" on the cover and spine is just marketing. It was a short-lived promotional club that no longer exists, and some later printings of the book remove mention of it entirely.

Leatherbound

ISBN	9781938570216
Release Year	2019
Publisher	Dragonsteel
Cover Price	100 USD
Cover Artist	Isaac Stewart
Estimated Value	$500 (800+ if numbered)

Arguably the prettiest of the leatherbound editions Dragonsteel has put out. The first printing has all the art printed on pearlescent paper, which gives it an absolutely gorgeous shine. Later printings do not have this pearlescent paper. Numbered edition prices spiked a few years ago with the craze from the secret projects Kickstarter, all the way up to $1500, but seem to have calmed down more recently.

The Stormlight Archive

Sanderson often refers to *Stormlight* as his "Magnum Opus", and it's easy to see why. The main novels are massive, and it's a planned 10-book series leading up to an enormous climax, with thousands of years of worldbuilding and an awesomely alien landscape. Plus, it has Kaladin and Adolin.

The Way of Kings Prime

Not a canonical part of *The Stormlight Archive*. This was Sanderson's first draft of the story, written back in 2004 or so, right before Elantris sold to

Tor/Moshe. It is fun to read just to see what elements ended up in the final book, and what changed.

US Hardcover

ISBN	9781938570247
Release Year	2020
Publisher	Dragonsteel
Cover Price	N/A
Cover Artist	Isaac Stewart
Estimated Value	$100

The first edition of this book only has one printing, and was released, unsigned, as part of the Kickstarter for the leatherbound edition of The Way of Kings. It was an add-on, and Dragonsteel printed enough copies to fulfill the Kickstarter pledges and not much more, so this book quickly became scarce and highly collectible.

It remains to be seen what will happen to the price over the next year, as there is a second edition coming with the Words of Radiance Kickstarter rewards, and so the story itself will become much more available for casual readers and collectors, leaving the first edition for the hardcore collectors, and hopefully freeing up a lot more supply.

At the time of writing, the price has already been dropping. Last year, copies sold quickly at $250. A copy is now sitting on eBay for $120 for over a day.

Altered Perceptions Hardcover

ISBN	N/A
Release Year	2014
Publisher	Fearful Symmetry
Cover Price	25.00 USD
Cover Artist	Robison Wells
Estimated Value	$75

This anthology was originally crowdfunded as a charity benefit. It contains several sample chapters from *The Way of Kings Prime*, and came out well before that hardcover.

The Way of Kings

The first novel in the *Stormlight Archive* series, and possibly the best-selling Sanderson book of all time. It is my favorite Sanderson book because it has the best example of leadership through adversity I have ever read

(Bridge 4), and it teaches that it's okay to be depressed, and you can still do awesome things.

ABM

ISBN	9780765326355
Release Year	2010
Publisher	Tor Books
Cover Price	N/A
Cover Artist	N/A
Estimated Value	$1500+

This was the last ABM of Sanderson's that Tor made. After this, his popularity was so high, and the publishing schedules so tight, that he got all the quotes and reviews that he needed to put on the books themselves, and there wasn't a long enough lead time to make an ABM.

White, slightly shorter than the trade paperback ARC, and with no cover art. The text inside is an earlier draft of the book, and lacks formatting from the final version.

ARC

ISBN	9780765326355
Release Year	2010
Publisher	Tor Books
Cover Price	N/A
Cover Artist	Michael Whelan
Estimated Value	$600

Probably the most common Cosmere ARC. This one pops up for sale fairly regularly on eBay.

Trade paperback sized with final cover art.

US Hardcover

ISBN	9780765326355
Release Year	2010
Publisher	Tor Books
Cover Price	27.99 USD / 31.99 CAN
Cover Artist	Michael Whelan
Estimated Value	$150-300

While one of the most desired Cosmere collectible books, this book also had a massive first print run. This book was released after Sanderson had already released his first book finishing *The Wheel of Time*, which had sold very well, and Tor knew that Sanderson was going to hit it big with his next solo book, as sales of all his other books had picked up. Thus, they printed a ton of these, and it is still not super hard to find. The value on these fluctuates a lot with the condition of the book.

The early printings of this book are thicker than the later printings, so you can tell with a glance at the shelf if something has a chance of being first printing or not. In addition, in the even later printings, the font was changed and the title is now vertical on the spine, instead of being horizontal.

If you're going for the best-looking set on your shelf, get the latest printing, as it matches the latest printing of *Words of Radiance*, and all printings of the later books, and it should not cost you more than cover price, as these are perpetually in print.

US Leatherbound

ISBN (Part 1)	9781938570223
ISBN (Part 2)	9781938570230
Release Year	2020
Publisher	Dragonsteel
Cover Price	200 USD
Cover Artist	Isaac Stewart
Estimated Value	$400+ ($900+ if numbered)

This book comes in two parts, but the parts are sold together in a single slipcase. They have separate ISBNs, and are separate books, but I have never seen any sold separately. All prices/values are for the pair.

The first printing of this book was sold through a Kickstarter campaign. The base signed hardcover was $200 for the slipcased pair. The numbered editions were $500, and came with a copy of *The Way of Kings Prime* as well as a massive amount of swag. Numbered editions were initially limited to 1000 copies, but Dragonsteel added another 1000 when the initial copies sold out very quickly.

There are three states of the first printing of this book, and they were shipped in two batches. The first batch shipped in 2020, and included the first 1000 numbered copies. The second batch, ordered by Dragonsteel when the first batch sold out, included the rest of the numbered copies and shipped in 2021. There were minor changes to the books, fixing fonts and typos and images, between the first and second batches, and partway through the printing of the second batch, a single typo was fixed, thus creating three states.

All numbered copies 1-1000 are first state, all numbered copies 1001-2000 are third state. There is generally not much price difference between the states that I have seen, but for handy reference, here is an identification guide.

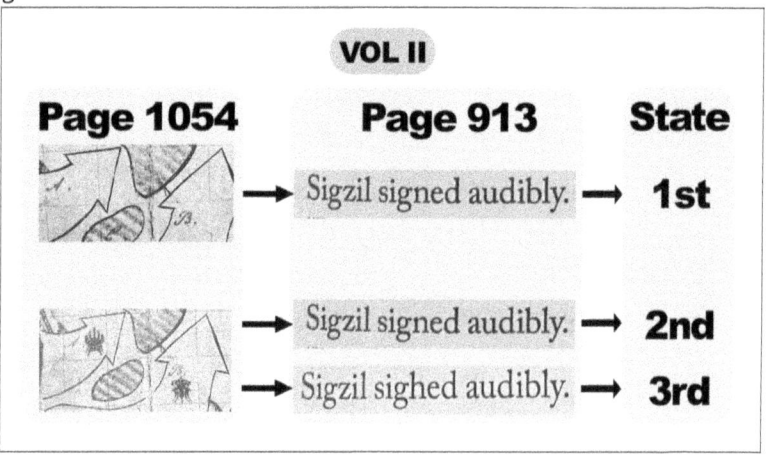

Page 1054	Page 913	State
	Sigzil signed audibly.	1st
	Sigzil signed audibly.	2nd
	Sigzil sighed audibly.	3rd

UK 1st edition Hardcover

ISBN	9780575099036
Release Year	2010
Publisher	Gollancz
Cover Price	20 GBP
Cover Artist	Sam Green
Estimated Value	$700+

While Gollancz realized Sanderson was big enough to have a hardcover, they did *not* print enough copies of this book. It's very rare, and excepting maybe numbered copies or ARCs, is the most valuable UK Sanderson collectible.

Be sure not to get this confused with the second UK Hardcover edition, released in 2021 with the ISBN 9781398703629. The first edition has the title at the top of the cover, and Sanderson's name at the bottom, while the second edition has it reversed. The second edition is still in print, and is only worth the cover price.

We have seen a very slight dip in the prices on this one with the release of the second edition, and it can sometimes be found under a thousand now, but is still quite pricey for a pristine copy, especially since many of the copies have bad page sag, discoloration, or other damage.

UK Sprayed Edge Hardcover

ISBN	9781399621199
Release Year	2023

Publisher	Gollancz
Cover Price	N/A
Cover Artist	Sam Green
Estimated Value	$50

While this one is relatively recent, and still in stock at the time of writing, Gollancz only ships copies to the UK, and so getting a copy to the US requires a re-shipper, which is why I have the value at slightly higher than the cover price.

It has red sprayed edges, with the first ideal of the Knights Radiant in white. All of the books in this set have a little silver ribbon bookmark.

UK Split Pocket Hardcovers

ISBN (part 1)	9781473233287
ISBN (part 2)	9781473233294
Release Year	2021
Publisher	Gollancz
Cover Price	16.99 GBP (each)
Cover Artist	Isaac Stewart
Estimated Value	$60 (pair)

These are generally sold as a pair. They are shorter blue casewrapped hardcovers, with the Windrunner glyph on the first part and the spears chapter icon for the second part.

Be careful if you buy this and want the true first that you get the ones that say 2021 on the copyright page. Gollancz lied to us by releasing a second state of both parts, with the same ISBNs, in 2022 (they did update that on the copyright page thankfully), and claiming that one is the first print as well. They reflowed the pages in this second state, making them have a higher pagecount. It's not something you can tell easily from an online posting, but holding the books side-by-side you can see the difference in thickness.

Fairyloot did "editions" of these, but they're literally just normal copies with yellow sprayed on the edges. No special endpapers, no separate ISBN, nothing. In my opinion these copies are overpriced (generally $100+) and don't even look better than the normal copies.

Mistborn/The Way of Kings Promo edition

ISBN	N/A
Release Year	2010
Publisher	Tor Books

Cover Price	N/A
Cover Artist	Michael Whelan
Estimated Value	$25

I am loathe to even put this book on the list. Back in 2015 or 2016, I worked as a volunteer at the Dragonsteel booth at GenCon. We had boxes and boxes of this promo, and were literally shoving them at anyone passing by who would take them. So many were given away for free, and it pains me to see that it is a little bit rare and collectible now, because I'm sure many of those copies got tossed in the trash.

This book has no ISBN and no number line, so I'm not sure if there were multiple print runs or not. All copies that I've seen have been identical.

Words of Radiance

This book was titled "The Book of Endless Pages" in draft, and Sanderson only changed the title because his publisher complained that the original was too on-the-nose for a 1000+ page fantasy novel. Lee Moyer made a great mock dust jacket of the book with that title, and last I checked, will still sell copies if you email his assistant through his website. However, as it's not an official/licensed item, I'm not including it in the guide.

The second book in the *Stormlight* series notoriously did not have an ARC. Production schedules were so tight that Tor instead sent out finished hardcovers, as soon as they came in off the presses, to reviewers instead. The production schedule was so insane that Peter Ahlstrom, Sanderson's editorial assistant, worked until he had to go to the hospital. Sanderson's team has vowed to never have such tight deadlines again.

US Hardcover

ISBN	9780765326362
Release Year	2014
Publisher	Tor Books
Cover Price	28.99 USD / 33.5 CAN
Cover Artist	Michael Whelan
Estimated Value	$80

A large print run, and being second in a series, make this generally more available than *The Way of Kings*.

This book suffers from the worst page sag I have seen in any US edition, and I highly recommend a book shoe if you are keeping your copy vertical on the shelf.

Later printings of this book follow a similar pattern to *The Way of Kings*, where the spine gets thinner, and then the font changes and the spine text goes vertical. Tor has an issue with the thinner printings of the hardcover, where the text and textboxes on the front and back of the book were never adjusted to be re-centered with the thinner spine, and so it looks unbalanced, especially on the back.

Additionally, the hardcover has not been updated with the new ending (though I am forever "Kaladin struck first"). I don't know if Tor ever plans to do that, or if that will be relegated to the paperbacks and leatherbound editions.

US Leatherbound

ISBN (Part 1)	9781938570308
ISBN (Part 2)	9781938570315
Release Year	2024
Publisher	Dragonsteel
Cover Price	250 USD
Cover Artist	Isaac Stewart
Estimated Value	$250

It was part of a BackerKit. The base book was $250 (and is again split into two parts, with a slipcase), and the numbered editions were $650, and included a copy of *Dragonsteel Prime* as well as *Secret Project 5* and lots of swag. These copies lasted a bit longer than the ones for *The Way of Kings*, but still sold out in the first hour after BackerKit recovered from the server crashes we gave them. There were 5,000 numbered copies, 4,898 of which were sold through the BackerKit. Presumably, the remaining 102 copies are for replacement of damaged books.

Despite the copyright page claiming a release date of December 2023, no copies of this book were shipped out until October 2024, so that is considered the actual release date.

UK Hardcover

ISBN	9780575099043
Release Year	2014
Publisher	Gollancz
Cover Price	20 GBP
Cover Artist	Sam Green
Estimated Value	$250+

While considerably more common than *The Way of Kings*, this UK edition is still rare and valuable, and was out of print for many years before the new sprayed edge editions were released.

UK Hardcover Sprayed Edges

ISBN	9781399621205
Release Year	2023
Publisher	Gollancz
Cover Price	N/A
Cover Artist	Sam Green
Estimated Value	$75

See notes on the UK Hardcover Sprayed Edges edition of *The Way of Kings*. The quote on this one is "WORDS ARE WHERE MOST CHANGE BEGINS." For some reason.

UK Split Pocket Hardcovers

ISBN (Part 1)	9781473233300
ISBN (Part 2)	9781473233317
Release Year	2022
Publisher	Gollancz
Cover Price	16.99 GBP (each)
Cover Artist	Isaac Stewart
Estimated Value	$40 (pair)

As far as I know, there was no second state of this book like there was with *The Way of Kings*. The covers are a gorgeous red color, and feature symbols from *Stormlight*: Lightweaver on part 1, and Pattern on part 2.

The same info as *The Way of Kings* applies here for the Fairyloot editions and these books being out of print.

Edgedancer

Edgedancer was first published in *Arcanum Unbounded*. See that book for more info.

US Pocket Hardcover

ISBN	9781250166548
Release Year	2016
Publisher	Tor Books
Cover Price	10.99 USD / 15.99 CAN

Cover Artist	Isaac Stewart
Estimated Value	$50

Beware of the fact that the 14th printing of this one accidentally had a full number line, a mistake I have confirmed through a contact at Tor. To find the true first printing, look at the spine. If there is a more square pattern with straight lines, as in the top of the picture below, it's an actual first (or other early) printing. If the designs are in a circular/hexagonal pattern, as in the bottom of the picture below, it's the fourteenth printing.

UK Pocket Hardcover

ISBN	9781473225039
Release Year	2018
Publisher	Gollancz
Cover Price	12.99 GBP
Cover Artist	Sam Green
Estimated Value	$40

In my opinion, the cover art on this one is even worse than the infamous "smoking Tress". Lift looks like she's wearing jeans, and the composition of the cover is clearly copied from Ben McSweeney's art that accompanied *Edgedancer* in *Arcanum Unbounded*.

Oathbringer

The third full volume in the *Stormlight Archive* series. By this point, Sanderson was a massive hit, and tons of numbered copies were sold at the release party. I was personally there and helping with the signing line. Sanderson started signing around 10 PM after his speech, and the signing line lasted until 4:27 AM (I still have the picture), when I was one of the the last people in the line.

Note that the ARC, US hardcover, and original UK hardcover all have a typo in the first printing. The table of contents refers to the book as "Book 2". This was not caught by the gamma readers because the table of contents was added in after the gamma read.

ARC

ISBN	9781250195104
Release Year	2017
Publisher	Tor Books
Cover Price	N/A
Cover Artist	Michael Whelan
Estimated Value	$1500+

There were only 100 of these ARCs made. To the best of my knowledge, the first 50 were signed and numbered by Sanderson.

US Hardcover

ISBN	9780765326379
Release Year	2017
Publisher	Tor Books
Cover Price	34.99 USD / 44.99 CAN
Cover Artist	Michael Whelan
Estimated Value	$60 ($300+ if numbered)

There are two states of this: the 10-line and the 0-line states. The only difference is the number line: In one, it starts "10 9 8", and in the other it's "0 9 8". All copies from the release party, including numbered editions, are 10-line. Outside of the numbered books, there is no difference in the value of these books, and most collectors won't care which one they have, much less try to get both of them, unless they're crazy like me. They are both considered true first printings and were released on the release date. Our best guess is that Tor sent very slightly different files to two different printing companies to order stock of the book.

UK Hardcover

ISBN	9780575093331
Release Year	2017

Publisher	Gollancz
Cover Price	25 GBP
Cover Artist	Sam Green
Estimated Value	$50

A relatively recent and highly printed UK edition. Also, these never went out of print, so later printings (and the sprayed edge edition) are still available. It's not worth much more than cover price.

UK Hardcover Sprayed Edges

ISBN	9781399621212
Release Year	2023
Publisher	Gollancz
Cover Price	N/A
Cover Artist	Sam Green
Estimated Value	$75

See notes on the UK Hardcover Sprayed Edges edition of *The Way of Kings*. The quote on this one is "PLAN EVERY BATTLE AS IF YOU WILL INEVITABLY RETREAT, BUT FIGHT EVERY BATTLE LIKE THERE IS NO BACKING DOWN."

UK Split Pocket Hardcovers

ISBN (Part 1)	9781473233324
ISBN (Part 2)	9781473233331
Release Year	2022
Publisher	Gollancz
Cover Price	16.99 GBP (each)
Cover Artist	Isaac Stewart
Estimated Value	$40 (pair)

The same notes apply here as for the *Words of Radiance* split hardcover, including Fairyloot and out of print. This is the worst-looking of these editions for me, because the pale yellow they chose is too pale and almost looks like the book is sun-stained, plus it's so light it stands out against the other editions.

Part 1 has the Bondsmith glyph on the cover, and Part 2 has the Kholin glyph chapter icon.

The Thrill (Oathbringer Excerpt in Unfettered 2)

This is just a few of Dalinar's flashback chapters that were released before *Oathbringer*'s official release as a kind of teaser.

"ARC"

ISBN	9781944145057
Release Year	2016
Publisher	Grim Oak Press
Cover Price	50 USD
Cover Artist	Todd Lockwood
Estimated Value	$40

One of Grim Oak's "ARC"s that does not meet the traditional definition of an ARC, this is a hardcover with a white background version of the cover art, and was sold publicly on Grim Oak's website. Lots of these were produced, and they stayed available on the web store for quite a while before selling out. The written cover price is $50, but they were sold for $20 on the web store. In addition, if I remember correctly, they came out after the regular hardcover did.

Hardcover

ISBN	9781944145057
Release Year	2016
Publisher	Grim Oak Press
Cover Price	35 USD
Cover Artist	Todd Lockwood
Estimated Value	$35

Tons were produced, demand is low.

Leatherbound Limited Edition

ISBN	9781944145057
Release Year	2021
Publisher	Grim Oak Press
Cover Price	200 USD
Cover Artist	Todd Lockwood
Estimated Value	$500

Came with a very nice slipcase, and wrap-around cover art with no text on the cover. This is a really pretty edition. It is signed to a tip-in page by all contributing authors, including Sanderson. Signing of the pages by all authors took an incredibly long time, thus the 2021 release date, while the original book came out in 2016.

Dawnshard

An awesome little novella that features a disabled protagonist, The Lopen finally learning some manners, and more Cosmere lore than some full novels.

Dragonsteel Pocket Hardcover

ISBN	9781938570254
Release Year	2021
Publisher	Dragonsteel
Cover Price	14.99 CAN / 18.99 CAN
Cover Artist	Ben McSweeney
Estimated Value	$40

The true first edition of the hardcover. Not very rare, but still worth a slight premium over the Tor edition. It was released as part of the *The Way of Kings* leatherbound Kickstarter.

The Tor edition has ISBN 9781250850553. In addition to the different publisher logos on the spine, you can identify the versions from the cover. On the Dragonsteel edition, the "E" in "SANDERSON" significantly overlaps with the circle around the larkin, with the bottom line below the outside of the circle, and the "D" and "R" on either side of it also overlap the circle. On the Tor edition, the bottom line of the "E" is directly on the edge of the circle, and the "D" and "R" hardly touch the very edge of the circle.

In the picture below, the Dragonsteel edition is on the left, and the Tor edition is on the right.

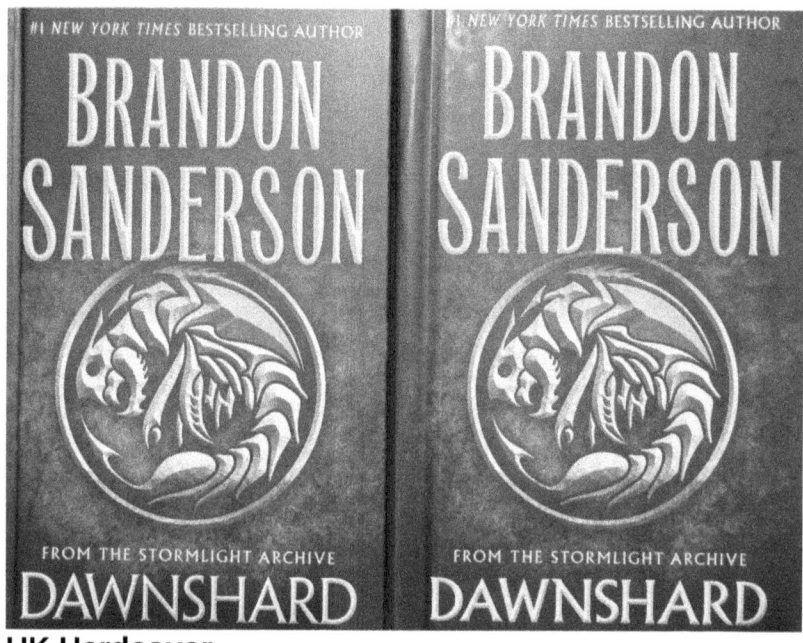

UK Hardcover

ISBN	9781803361062
Release Year	2022
Publisher	Titan Books
Cover Price	9.99 GBP
Cover Artist	Julia Lloyd
Estimated Value	$15

Unlike nearly all of Sanderson's other UK books, this one was published by Titan Books, and unlike all the other smaller format hardcovers, it has a dust jacket instead of being casewrapped. Rumor has it that Gollancz wouldn't agree to the audiobook terms that Sanderson wanted, so he took the book elsewhere. This is also why the book doesn't have a Sam Green cover, although Lloyd's style does match pretty well.

Rhythm of War

The fourth book in *The Stormlight Archive*. They just keep getting longer and more awesome. The scientific magical aspects of this one are absolutely entrancing, and I adore it.

ARC

ISBN	9781250810489

Release Year	2020
Publisher	Tor Books
Cover Price	34.99 USD / 44.99 CAD
Cover Artist	Michael Whelan
Estimated Value	$2000+

This Tor ARC actually has a separate ISBN from the final book, something they have only done for Sanderson once or twice. Once again, I believe about 100 were produced, and half were signed and numbered by Sanderson.

US Hardcover

ISBN	9780765326386
Release Year	2020
Publisher	Tor Books
Cover Price	34.99 USD / 44.99 CAD
Cover Artist	Michael Whelan
Estimated Value	$35

As a pandemic release, all numbered copies of this one were sold online, and there was no release party. It was the first in an exciting new trend from Dragonsteel: all numbered copies are numbered inside a stamp, authenticating the fact that the book was numbered.

UK Hardcover

ISBN	9780575093386
Release Year	2020
Publisher	Gollancz
Cover Price	25 GBP
Cover Artist	Sam Green
Estimated Value	$40

Still easily available.

UK Hardcover Sprayed Edges

ISBN	9781399621229
Release Year	2023
Publisher	Gollancz
Cover Price	N/A
Cover Artist	Sam Green
Estimated Value	$75

See notes on the UK Hardcover Sprayed Edges edition of *The Way of Kings*. The quote on this one is "FEW MEN HAVE THE WISDOM TO REALIZE WHEN THEY NEED HELP. FEWER STILL HAVE THE STRENGTH TO GO GET IT."

UK Split Pocket Hardcovers

ISBN (Part 1)	9781473233379
ISBN (Part 2)	9781473233386
Release Year	2023
Publisher	Gollancz
Cover Price	16.99 GBP (each)
Cover Artist	Isaac Stewart
Estimated Value	$40 (pair)

Same notes as *Words of Radiance* and *Oathbringer* in this edition apply. It's a gorgeous purple color, and the last one that Gollancz is doing, unfortunately. There will be no corresponding *Wind and Truth* edition, as they have switched to doing the one-volume paperbacks instead.

Both parts have the Willshaper glyph on the cover, making this the only installment that doesn't have separate art for each part.

Wind and Truth

The fifth volume, this marks the end of an era, similar to the end of Mistborn Era One. We know that there will be a time gap (both in-world and in writing time) before the final five volumes are written and released.

US Hardcover

ISBN	9781250319180
Release Year	2024
Publisher	Tor Books
Cover Price	39.99 USD
Cover Artist	Michael Whelan
Estimated Value	$40

Sanderson signed 15,000 copies of this book for release, but they were all tip-in pages. Of these, 10,000 were numbered for the release party. ~6,000 of these were sold for pickup at Dragonsteel Nexus 2024, and the other ~4,000 were sold online. All numbered copies came as part of a bundle with a chull plushie, an epic bookmark, and a Szeth pin, which cost $80. The 4,000 on the Dragonsteel Books online store sold out in under an hour. The signed, unnumbered copies had a separate ISBN and are listed below.

And yes, the numbered release party copies are signed to a tip-in. This is probably something we can expect for most release party books going forward, simply because it's much easier for Sanderson to sign them, and for the publisher to ship just the tip-in pages around.

US Hardcover Signed Tip-in

ISBN	9781250387202
Release Year	2024
Publisher	Tor Books
Cover Price	39.99 USD
Cover Artist	Michael Whelan
Estimated Value	$75

See above.

UK Hardcover

ISBN	9781399601313
Release Year	2024
Publisher	Gollancz
Cover Price	30 GBP
Cover Artist	Sam Green
Estimated Value	$45

There were no numbered copies of this one, but Waterstones did a signed tip-in edition and a separate sprayed edges edition, which are below.

UK Hardcover Signed Tip-in

ISBN	9781399630467
Release Year	2024
Publisher	Gollancz
Cover Price	30 GBP
Cover Artist	Sam Green
Estimated Value	$75

Likely signed to a tip-in page. These sold out within a day of being listed.

UK Hardcover Sprayed Edges

ISBN	9781399628556
Release Year	2024
Publisher	Gollancz

Cover Price	30 GBP
Cover Artist	Sam Green
Estimated Value	$55

This is a Waterstones edition and does not match the Gollancz sprayed edge editions of books 1-4. The art is red and shows what appears to be a sunrise over the mountains. Price is slightly higher just to accommodate shipping from the UK.

The Stormlight Archive Pocket Companion

Released as a one-off as a promotional item for Indie Bookstore Day in 2016, this very short (32-page) book contains a small world guide to Roshar, including some artwork, and was the first book to hint at the existence of The Sibling.

US Casewrapped Hardcover

ISBN	9780765391674
Release Year	2016
Publisher	Tor
Cover Price	N/A
Cover Artist	Isaac Stewart
Estimated Value	$125

Despite initially being free, copies of this were relatively scare and difficult to get, and it has become very collectible.

Kaladin Art Book

Originally released as part of the Kickstarter for the Kaladin music album, a "book soundtrack" to accompany *The Way of Kings*. That campaign, run by The Black Piper, barely funded, and the art book was stuck in development hell for years before being finished.

Hardcover

ISBN	N/A
Release Year	2022
Publisher	The Black Piper
Cover Price	N/A
Cover Artist	Grant M. Hansen
Estimated Value	$40

Black Piper majorly overproduced these books, and I was sent several boxes of copies with minor blemishes that were left over. I have brought these copies to several conventions, including previous Dragonsteel events, and given them to the SCG to sell at $40 each. I will be out soon, but for the moment these are not rare.

Paperback

ISBN	N/A
Release Year	2021
Publisher	The Black Piper
Cover Price	N/A
Cover Artist	Grant M. Hansen
Estimated Value	$50

These copies were sold by Black Piper at a convention or two *before* the Kickstarter "exclusive" hardcover was actually shipped out, and so they're technically the first published edition. However, they are not highly sought after due to the hardcover existing.

White Sand

Sand. Singular. I really wish people would stop calling this "White Sands".

This story was originally written as a prose book, one of the first that Sanderson ever wrote. After it was a trunk novel for many years, Dynamite picked it up and gave it a graphic novel treatment, which took several years and went through two artist changes. The full three volumes of the graphic novel tell the approximate full story of the prose novel. We hope to get a revised canon version of the prose novel some day, but until then, we have the graphic novel.

White Sand 1

A short excerpt from this did appear in *Arcanum Unbounded*.

Hardcover

ISBN	9781606908853
Release Year	2016
Publisher	Dynamite Entertainment
Cover Price	24.99 USD
Cover Artist	Julius Gopez
Estimated Value	$100

Prices on this one were high for a while because it was out-of-print, but with the release of the omnibus and newer printings, it has come back down.

Signed Tip-in

ISBN	9781524102555
Release Year	2016
Publisher	Dynamite Entertainment
Cover Price	39.99 USD
Cover Artist	Julius Gopez
Estimated Value	$75

An interesting anomaly. This book *only* appears in the second printing. It is signed to a tip-in page, and has a distinct ISBN, and was sold by Dynamite, so it's a legitimate edition, but apparently they sold out of the first printing before putting the tip-in pages in, and had to do it on the second printing.

White Sand 2

The artist changes partway through this book, because the first artist couldn't keep up with all the deadlines, and it's a fairly jarring change. Even looking at just the page edges, you can see that the new artist uses art that goes to the edge of the page way more often. I find the new art style a lot cleaner and easier to follow as well.

Hardcover

ISBN	9781524103422
Release Year	2018
Publisher	Dynamite Entertainment
Cover Price	24.99 USD
Cover Artist	Julius Gopez
Estimated Value	$50

Dynamite seems to have produced this one in much higher quantities than volume 1, and it is not very rare.

Signed Tip-in

ISBN	9781524103460
Release Year	2018
Publisher	Dynamite Entertainment
Cover Price	39.99 USD
Cover Artist	Julius Gopez

Estimated Value	$60

Again, not terribly hard to find. Thankfully this one is a first printing.

White Sand 3

Hardcover

ISBN	9781524110062
Release Year	2019
Publisher	Dynamite Entertainment
Cover Price	24.99 USD
Cover Artist	Fritz Casas
Estimated Value	$30

If you're patient, you can find this one even cheaper. It's not hard to find at all.

Signed Tip-in

ISBN	9781524112936
Release Year	2019
Publisher	Dynamite Entertainment
Cover Price	39.99 USD
Cover Artist	Fritz Casas
Estimated Value	$40

Again, thankfully this one is a first printing.

White Sand Omnibus

In addition to containing all of the art from the three volumes in the series, this includes an extra prologue that focuses on Khriss, which is good because she's supposed to be the main character, not just Kenton. In addition, a lot of the "sand" scratches in the art style were cleaned up, and a some of the worst art (boombox) was redone or retouched. There is also a very short epilogue added to this edition. Fatooom.

If you want a version of the story for reading, definitely get the omnibus.

Deluxe Glitter Hardcover

ISBN (signed)	9781524122690
ISBN (unsigned)	9781524122591
Release Year	2023

Publisher	Dynamite Entertainment
Cover Price	N/A
Cover Artist	Dan Dos Santos
Estimated Value	$80

The "signed" edition of this book is not actually signed. They shipped with a bookplate, no signature in the actual book. There are no distinguishing features between the two, as both ISBNs are printed on the copyright page.

Dynamite affixed all of the bookplates that came with this book to a separate piece of paper. So you can't even take them and insert them into the book. It is one of the most baffling and frustrating decisions that I have ever seen a publisher make.

In addition, printing this book was an absolute nightmare for Dynamite. The first print run was entirely discarded for quality issues. The second print run started being shipped out, and people complained that the shiny silver on the cover was shedding so bad it looked like glitter. Dynamite stopped the shipping, ordered the copies reprinted, and shipped out copies including to everyone who had a glitter-bomb copy. They sent mailing labels for everyone with the glitter copies to send them back to Dragonsteel, where they still lurk on the Darkside.

Casewrapped Hardcover

ISBN	9781524122577
Release Year	2023
Publisher	Dynamite Entertainment
Cover Price	70.00 USD
Cover Artist	Nabetse Zitro and Justyna Dura
Estimated Value	$70

Still available via Dynamite and Amazon. I have not yet seen a second printing at the time of writing.

Other Planets

Shadows for Silence in the Forests of Hell

A delightfully dark story set on the planet of Threnody, this one originally appeared as part of *Dangerous Women*, an anthology headlined by George R. R. Martin. This story is also part of *Arcanum Unbounded*.

Due to its extraordinarily long name, it is often referred to by the rather silly acronym SfSitFoH, which I personally pronounce "Siff sit foe". We can't just call it "Shadows", because that's already taken by *Shadows of Self*.

Dangerous Women ARC

ISBN	9780765332066
Release Year	2013
Publisher	Tor Books
Cover Price	N/A
Cover Artist	N/A
Estimated Value	$1500+

One of the rarest and hardest to find Sanderson ARCs, because this book also contains a story by George R. R. Martin, an author who is more famous and less prolific than Sanderson.

White, trade paperback size, with no cover art.

Dangerous Women US Hardcover

ISBN	9780765332066
Release Year	2013
Publisher	Tor Books
Cover Price	32.50 USD / 37.50 CAN
Cover Artist	N/A
Estimated Value	$35

No, I'm not neglecting the data. This book simply does not credit a cover artist.

As a book with GRRM in it, this had a massive first print run, and is still quite easy to find.

Dangerous Women UK Hardcover

ISBN	9780007549405
Release Year	2013
Publisher	Harper Voyager UK
Cover Price	20 GBP
Cover Artist	Royal Armories
Estimated Value	$30

At least this one credits a cover artist, even if it is just a graphic design company.

SfSitFoH/Perfect State Sub Press Lettered

ISBN	N/A
Release Year	2015
Publisher	Subterranean Press
Cover Price	275 USD
Cover Artist	Tom Kidd
Estimated Value	$1500+

This is two volumes in a traycase, limited to 26 copies. (Though I have also seen at least one PC copy.) No copies have been sold that I know of in quite a while. This is one of the handful of books that I still need, so if you have a copy, please let me know!

SfSitFoH/Perfect State Sub Press Numbered

ISBN	N/A
Release Year	2015
Publisher	Subterranean Press
Cover Price	99 USD
Cover Artist	Tom Kidd
Estimated Value	$550

This is two volumes in a slipcase. Both volumes are signed and numbered. Estimated value is from a recent eBay auction. There were 500 numbered copies.

SfSitFoH/Perfect State Con Double

ISBN	9781938570063
Release Year	2015
Publisher	Dragonsteel
Cover Price	20 USD
Cover Artist	Miranda Meeks and J.P. Targete
Estimated Value	$150

A con double. The two stories are printed in one volume, upside-down from each other, so that you can start at either end of the book and read one story. The middle of the three con doubles that Dragonsteel released, this book had a high print run, but has been sold out and is out of print. It is also the easiest way to get *Perfect State* in English before next year's non-Cosmere anthology, making this one quite desirable.

Miranda Meeks' art is on the *Shadows* side, and Targete's is on the *Perfect State* side.

Two Cosmere Fragments

Two little storylets: One a first draft of a scene involving a proto-Wayne talking to his horse, who happens to be a kandra. That idea got completely reworked and scrapped in the creation of Mistborn Era Two. And second, a brief conversation between Hoid and Frost, taking place right after Mistborn Era One. This second is available as *The Traveler* for free on Sanderson's website. There is only one place to find these in print: the JordanCon 2019 charity anthology, *You Want Stories?*. And yes, the title has a question mark in it.

You Want Stories? ARC

ISBN	9781091599314
Release Year	2019
Publisher	JordanCon
Cover Price	20 USD
Cover Artist	Dan Dos Santos
Estimated Value	$201

Only five copies of this were produced, and they were true "proof" copies instead of being ARCs. They were distributed among the JordanCon staff who produced the anthology. One copy was reserved for the JordanCon charity auction, where I bought it in 2024, which is where the (somewhat facetious) estimated value comes from.

You Want Stories? Paperback

ISBN	9781091599314
Release Year	2019
Publisher	JordanCon
Cover Price	20 USD
Cover Artist	Dan Dos Santos
Estimated Value	$25

JordanCon way over-ordered these books. I personally bought 20 of them the year it came out, and still have probably half of them that I will sell if anyone needs one. The SCG also bought some copies at one point, and we sell them at the booth.

Tress of the Emerald Sea

Sanderson's retelling of *The Princess Bride*, except when Wesley is captured, Buttercup boards a ship and sails off to save him. It is told in a delightful fairy tale manner, and features a ton of amazing lines.

Dragonsteel Deluxe Hardcover

ISBN	9781938570322
Release Year	2023
Publisher	Dragonsteel
Cover Price	55 USD
Cover Artist	Howard Lyon
Estimated Value	$55

First prints are still readily available through the Dragonsteel store. Dragonsteel printed ~150,000 copies of each of the secret projects, and they will not be rare for a long time.

Only 50 copies were numbered of this book. #1 went to Emily (Brandon's wife), #2-5 were reserved for artists and other contributors, and the other 45 numbers went to students in Sanderson's BYU class in Spring 2023. None have come up for sale yet, but it is assumed that if they do, they will be quite expensive.

US Tor Hardcover

ISBN	9781250899651
Release Year	2023
Publisher	Tor Books
Cover Price	29.99 USD
Cover Artist	Carlos Guimerá
Estimated Value	$40

This book had a considerably lower print run than the Dragonsteel edition, but sold really well upon release, surprising Tor and everyone else. It quickly went through several printings, and I saw at least 7th printings within a year of release. Purely due to this, it is slightly collectible, though most collectors still prefer the Dragonsteel edition, and if you are patient buying online you can find a copy fairly easily/cheaply.

UK Hardcover

ISBN	9781399613378
Release Year	2023

Publisher	Gollancz
Cover Price	22 GBP
Cover Artist	Sam Green
Estimated Value	$50

Ahhh, the infamous "smoking Tress" cover. Dragonsteel has publicly stated (on Reddit) that they dislike this cover. It is likely this cover is part of the reason that the other 3 secret projects used the US cover art, instead of Sam Green cover art. Gollancz quietly redacted this cover and replaced it with the US cover art, somewhere around the 3rd printing of this hardcover, with the same ISBN.

Yumi and the Nightmare Painter

The third of the secret projects that made up Sanderson's #1 Kickstarter of all time. This is a body-swap ghost mentor story about art and self-worth. For many fans, it is their favorite of the secret projects.

UK ARC

ISBN	9781399613439
Release Year	2023
Publisher	Gollancz
Cover Price	N/A
Cover Artist	N/A
Estimated Value	$1100

There are no US ARCs of any of the secret projects, but UK ARCs have turned up for *Yumi* and *Frugal Wizard*. I have not been able to get a response from the UK publicist to confirm how many of these were made, or how they were distributed. The only copy we have seen was sent to a UK bookseller as a review copy. The value is the approximate price I paid in trade value to get that one copy.

It has a black cover with no cover art, and is significantly shorter than a normal ARC.

Dragonsteel Deluxe Hardcover

ISBN	9781938570377
Release Year	2023
Publisher	Dragonsteel
Cover Price	55 USD
Cover Artist	Aliya Chen

| Estimated Value | $55 |

Like the other secret projects, has a print run of ~150,000 and is still in stock on the Dragonsteel store at the time of writing.

Also only has 50 numbered copies, with numbers 1-5 reserved for Emily and the artists. Some numbers were given out to fans at conventions, if you knew the right person to ask.

US Tor Hardcover

ISBN	9781250899699
Release Year	2023
Publisher	Tor Books
Cover Price	29.99 USD
Cover Artist	Tran Nguyen
Estimated Value	$35

First prints are even easier to find than for Tress, but the book has still moved on to later printings, so you have to look a bit to be sure you find one.

UK Hardcover

ISBN	9781399613439
Release Year	2023
Publisher	Gollancz
Cover Price	22 GBP
Cover Artist	Tran Nguyen
Estimated Value	$35

The UK hardcover has the same cover art as the US Tor edition.

UK Hardcover Sprayed Edges

ISBN	9781399623018
Release Year	2023
Publisher	Gollancz
Cover Price	22 GBP
Cover Artist	Tran Nguyen
Estimated Value	$50

This edition was sold by Waterstones in the UK, not directly by Gollancz. It was, however, cleared with Dragonsteel, and is considered an official edition. In fact, it is the first official sprayed edge edition that is not a leatherbound. The sprayed edges are blue, with a white flower/vine pattern on them. The pattern doesn't really have anything to do with the story itself, but it is pretty, and I am so happy that we are starting to get sprayed edge editions of Sanderson's works.

The Sunlit Man

This book is special to me because it is the secret project that I beta read. (Each of us only got one of the four books.) It features a character from *Stormlight* but far into the future. In my opinion, it is best read after *Wind and Truth*.

Dragonsteel Deluxe Hardcover

ISBN	9781938570391
Release Year	2023
Publisher	Dragonsteel
Cover Price	$55
Cover Artist	Kudriaken
Estimated Value	$55

Like the other secret projects, this book had a printing of ~150,000, and is still in stock on the Dragonsteel store. Also like the others, it had 50 numbered copies, #1 going to Emily, #2-5 being given to artists, and others being given out at conventions. I got a number by standing in the number line very early at the Defiant release party.

US Tor Hardcover

ISBN	9781250899712
Release Year	2024
Publisher	Tor Books
Cover Price	29.99 USD
Cover Artist	Danny Schlitz
Estimated Value	$35

I really like Danny Schlitz's art, after seeing what he did with the *Mistborn* books and now here, and I hope that Tor/Sanderson brings him back for future books.

UK Hardcover

ISBN	9781399613460
Release Year	2024
Publisher	Gollancz
Cover Price	22 GBP
Cover Artist	Danny Schlitz

| Estimated Value | $40 |

No notes.

UK Hardcover Sprayed Edges

ISBN	9781399625906
Release Year	2024
Publisher	Gollancz
Cover Price	22 GBP
Cover Artist	Danny Schlitz
Estimated Value	$55

Unlike the regular hardcovers, this one is out of stock and becoming rarer. The sprayed edges are full color, with an orange sun and a brilliant red background, and the imagery is actually relevant to the book.

Dragonsteel Prime

Non-canon story that is an early introduction to Hoid and Frost, both of whom exchange letters in the *Stormlight* epigraphs. You can read it for free on Sanderson's website, as it has been released as a curiosity.

US Hardcover

ISBN	9781938570483
Release Year	2024
Publisher	Dragonsteel
Cover Price	45 USD
Cover Artist	Jian Guo
Estimated Value	$45

This book was sold as part of the BackerKit for the *Words of Radiance* leatherbound. It only arrived during the writing of this book, and it remains to be seen how many extra copies Dragonsteel (the company) printed and will have available before the first print run runs out.

Anthologies

Despite claiming that he cannot write short stories because they always turn into novels, Sanderson has a number of Cosmere shorts published in various places, though most of them are collected in *Arcanum Unbounded*.

Sixth of the Dusk

My least favorite Cosmere story. The ending just isn't satisfying to me, and shifts the focus of the story majorly just to go "oooh, Cosmere." I am hopeful it is improved by whatever is in *Secret Project 5*. It is also included in *Arcanum Unbounded*, below.

Shadows Beneath US Hardcover

ISBN	9781938570032
Release Year	2014
Publisher	Dragonsteel
Cover Price	25 USD
Cover Artist	Julie Dillon
Estimated Value	$100 (numbered $250+)

There are 200 signed and numbered copies, with signatures from all 4 contributing authors.

This anthology includes some very cool behind the scenes stuff, as it includes the original Writing Excuses episodes where the story was brainstormed, as well as the first draft of the story, the revision episode of Writing Excuses, and the final story.

Arcanum Unbounded

An anthology of all of Sanderson's Cosmere short fiction published up through 2016. The main reason it is collectible is because it is the first published edition of *Edgedancer*, a *Stormlight* novella. The Cosmere star charts and notes about each system are new as well, but the rest of the stories are reprints from various places.

ARC

ISBN	9780765391162
Release Year	2016
Publisher	Tor Books
Cover Price	N/A
Cover Artist	N/A
Estimated Value	$2000+

Seemingly one of the hardest Cosmere ARCs to find. This one is highly sought after, including by multiple collectors with resources to spare. White trade paperback with no cover art.

US Hardcover

ISBN	9780765391162
Release Year	2016
Publisher	Tor Books
Cover Price	27.99 USD / 38.99 CAN
Cover Artist	David Palumbo
Estimated Value	$75

Slightly rare as a 1/1, though if you're patient you can snag a good copy on eBay in less than a month usually.

UK Hardcover

ISBN	9781473218031
Release Year	2016
Publisher	Gollancz
Cover Price	16.99 GBP
Cover Artist	Sam Green
Estimated Value	$75

Same as the US hardcover. Note not to be fooled by the UK casewrapped hardcover, ISBN 9781473225930, which is much smaller, was released later, and is not collectible.

Collectible Books - Non-Cosmere

Despite being most well-known for writing the Cosmere, Sanderson has written a lot of books and stories in other settings as well. Most of his other settings involve Earth in some form or another, and the Cosmere will never have Earth in it.

Star's End

I feel a little mean including this book here, but I would be remiss not to mention it. *Star's End* is the second book that Sanderson ever wrote, after *White Sand Prime*. It has never been published. In 2007, he asked Isaac Stewart to use a print-on-demand service to print up copies for Sanderson's personal collection, as a vanity item. Isaac did this, as well as printing copies for himself.

I forget exactly when I saw them in Sanderson's collection, but I asked him and Isaac about them, and was given permission to pay Isaac to print another set (hardcover and paperback) for my personal collection.

A few years later, the Sanderson Collectors Guild asked for permission and were granted another 30 pairs. Each of these went to a guild member who had been around for a long time, and I received one pair of this set as well, making me the only collector with two pairs. As far as I know, there are only 33 copies in existence of each format, and all of the pairs are together.

None has ever come up for sale, nor should they ever. All of us who got copies agreed never to sell them.

Hardcover

ISBN	9780368339257
Release Year	2007
Publisher	Dragonsteel
Cover Price	N/A
Cover Artist	Isaac Stewart
Estimated Value	N/A

The hardcover has a marbled blue cover with a 16-pointed star. To the best of my knowledge, that symbol has no relation to Adonalsium/the Cosmere.

Paperback

ISBN	9780368339189

Release Year	2007
Publisher	Dragonsteel
Cover Price	N/A
Cover Artist	Isaac Stewart
Estimated Value	N/A

The paperback cover shows a spaceship flying in front of a nebula of some sort.

Alcatraz

When Sanderson initially wrote and began publishing this series, during the same time Mistborn Era One was releasing, he wasn't sure if his career would ultimately end up being in middle grade like this, or epic fantasy, like the Cosmere. We are very lucky that it ended up being the Cosmere, but *Alcatraz* is an absolutely delightful and criminally underrated series, and so far it's the only Sanderson series I have been able to get my kid into.

Alcatraz vs. The Evil Librarians

This book has three main publications, and each publication has an associated ARC, giving this book the most official ARCs of any book (though *Steelheart* overtakes it with ABMs). Only the first publication as a hardcover by Scholastic is collectible, the later Starscape hardcover and Starscape paperback are generally not sought out. Starscape is Tor's sister middle grade publishing imprint. It has a UK paperback.

Scholastic ARC

ISBN	9780439925501
Release Year	2007
Publisher	Scholastic
Cover Price	N/A
Cover Artist	Marc Tauss
Estimated Value	$100-300

Despite being an early Sanderson ARC with probably a relatively low printing, because this is part of a criminally underrated series, it is one of the cheaper ARCs.

First Starscape ARC

| ISBN | 9780765378941 |
| Release Year | 2016 |

Publisher	Starscape
Cover Price	N/A
Cover Artist	Scott Brundage
Estimated Value	$80

    This one is interesting, because it lists the title in a completely different font/style than ended up on the actual book, and it lists the title as "*Alcatraz versus the Evil Librarians*", while the corresponding hardcover instead says "vs".

    This was released for the original Starscape hardcover run. After Sanderson had bought the Alcatraz series rights back from Scholastic, Starscape bought them and rereleased the first four books, and released book five. None of the other first four books got a new ARC.

Second Starscape ARC

ISBN	9781250860286
Release Year	2022
Publisher	Starscape
Cover Price	N/A
Cover Artist	Justin Gerard
Estimated Value	$70

    Fire over the inheritance! This is the only ARC besides *The Emperor's Soul* that I can think of that is for a paperback release. It was released when Starscape re-released the first five books in the series in paperback with new covers leading up to Bastille's release. It was the only one of the five that got a new ARC.

Scholastic Hardcover

ISBN	9780439925501
Release Year	2007
Publisher	Scholastic Press
Cover Price	16.99 USD / 20.99 CAN
Cover Artist	Marc Tauss
Estimated Value	$75

    The only reason this one holds any value is that completionists and people with exceptionally good taste will collect it. Anyone who wants to read the book should get one of the Starscape editions. Hayley Lazo's illustrations elevate the book so much, and are essential to the experience.

UK Paperback

ISBN	9781444006681
Release Year	2013
Publisher	Gollancz
Cover Price	6.99 GBP
Cover Artist	Patrick Knowles
Estimated Value	$25

I hesitated to add these editions, but they're the first (and only) UK edition of this book, though it did also appear in the *"Complete" Alcatraz*.

The Scrivener's Bones

This book has three major editions as well: Scholastic, Starscape hardcover, and Starscape paperback. Only the Scholastic is considered collectible, and that is also the only one with an ARC.

That original Scholastic release had a cover supposedly depicting Alcatraz on the Dragonaut, but the art was so campy/inaccurate that it is one of Sanderson's least favorite covers, and he made fun of it in the next book in the series (and somehow got away with the publisher letting him do it).

ARC

ISBN	9780439925532
Release Year	2008
Publisher	Scholastic Press
Cover Price	N/A
Cover Artist	Marc Tauss
Estimated Value	$100

Slightly rarer than the first book, but still not desired by many collectors.

Scholastic Hardcover

ISBN	9780439925532
Release Year	2008
Publisher	Scholastic Press
Cover Price	16.99 USD / 18.99 CAN
Cover Artist	Marc Tauss
Estimated Value	$80

Like book one, if you want to read a copy, get the Starscape version with the Hayley Lazo illustrations. Only collect this if you want true firsts.

UK Paperback

ISBN	9781444006698
Release Year	2013
Publisher	Gollancz
Cover Price	6.99 GBP
Cover Artist	Patrick Knowles
Estimated Value	$15

I hesitated to add these editions, but they're the first (and only) UK edition of this book.

The Knights of Crystallia

You know the drill. Three releases at three points in time, but only an ARC for the first one.

ARC

ISBN	9780439925556
Release Year	2024
Publisher	Scholastic Press
Cover Price	16.99 USD / 21.99 CAD
Cover Artist	Marc Tauss
Estimated Value	$1500

The surprisingly high value on this one comes from its unexplained rarity. We only know of two copies, one of which is in my collection and was found at a thrift shop in the middle of nowhere Wisconsin by a guy from Israel, and sold for $0.50. (Thank you so much, Ari.) No, I didn't misplace a decimal point. 50 cents is what the shop sold it for. I paid a finder's fee proportionate to the book costing $1500, and I know a few very prominent collectors for whom this is one of only a handful of ARCs they are missing.

Scholastic Hardcover

ISBN	9780439925556
Release Year	2009
Publisher	Scholastic Press
Cover Price	16.99 USD / 21.99 CAN
Cover Artist	Marc Tauss
Estimated Value	$100

It's possible that Sanderson's sales hit a bit of a slump around this point in the series, and Scholastic didn't print as many copies, which would explain the relative rarity of both the ARC and the hardcover on this one.

UK Paperback

ISBN	9781444006704
Release Year	2013
Publisher	Gollancz
Cover Price	6.99 GBP
Cover Artist	Patrick Knowles
Estimated Value	$100?

Bizarrely hard to find, just like the US editions of this book. If you want the UK set, search for this one first.

The Shattered Lens

The last book in the "original" Alcatraz series, as published by Scholastic. It has the same three main editions as the first four, with an ARC for the Scholastic release.

ARC

ISBN	9780439925570
Release Year	2010
Publisher	Scholastic Press
Cover Price	N/A
Cover Artist	Marc Tauss
Estimated Value	$200

While this one does appear to be more rare than books one and two, it's definitely easier to find than *Crystallia*, and being an Alcatraz ARC, it has a correspondingly low value.

Scholastic Hardcover

ISBN	9780439925570
Release Year	2010
Publisher	Scholastic Press
Cover Price	17.99 USD / 22.99 CAN
Cover Artist	Marc Tauss
Estimated Value	$75

As always, this is for collectors of firsts. Get the Starscape edition for the illustrations if you want to read.

UK Paperback

ISBN	9781444006711
Release Year	2013
Publisher	Gollancz
Cover Price	6.99 GBP
Cover Artist	Patrick Knowles
Estimated Value	$15

I hesitated to add these editions, but they're the first (and only) UK edition of this book.

The Complete Alcatraz

This book is a UK-only bindup that is very much not complete. It only contains the first four books, and was only released in paperback.

Paperback

ISBN	9780575131347
Release Year	2012
Publisher	Gollancz
Cover Price	16.99 GBP
Cover Artist	Sam Green
Estimated Value	$20

Easy to find used on Amazon and the like. I only included it here because it is a unique/interesting edition, being the only English language book to contain multiple other books that Sanderson considers complete novels.

The Dark Talent

A long time after the first four books were released and Scholastic dropped the series, Sanderson bought the rights back and after becoming much more popular, resold them to Starscape, Tor's sister middle grade publishing imprint. There are two main editions of this one, one from the hardcover release, and one from the paperback release when Bastille came out. There is an ARC of the hardcover release. This book has been released in a few translations, but has never been published in the UK.

ARC

ISBN	9780765381408
Release Year	2016
Publisher	Starscape

Cover Price	N/A
Cover Artist	Scott Brundage
Estimated Value	$75

Quite common and not commonly collected.

Starscape Hardcover

ISBN	9780765381408
Release Year	2016
Publisher	Starscape
Cover Price	16.99 USD / 23.99 CAN
Cover Artist	Scott Brundage
Estimated Value	$25

Tons were produced, and they are still very easy to find with even just a little patience.

Bastille vs. The Evil Librarians

After Starscape released the first five books, Sanderson hit a bit of a writing block on this one, and it wasn't until Janci Patterson took over and owned the voice of Bastille that a draft was finished and published. The time gap was great enough that Starscape rereleased the first five books in paperback leading up to the publication of this one. While it has come out in Spanish, I have seen no other translations, and there is no UK edition.

ARC

ISBN	9781250876904
Release Year	2022
Publisher	Starscape
Cover Price	17.99 USD / 23.99 CAD
Cover Artist	Justin Gerard
Estimated Value	$45

The most over-produced Sanderson ARC of all time. Massive numbers were printed and handed out liberally, including a box that went directly to collectors. If you're looking for a starter ARC or a gateway drug, this is where you go. At one point I had five copies, before giving them to friends.

Starscape Hardcover

| ISBN | 9781250811066 |
| Release Year | 2022 |

Publisher	Starscape
Cover Price	17.99 USD / 23.99 CAN
Cover Artist	Justin Gerard
Estimated Value	$18

Insanely easy to find, even for the triple-signed (Janci, Hayley, and Sanderson) stamped and numbered edition which was still available in the Dragonsteel Books store for at least a year after the book was released. At the time of writing, they have triple-signed (but not numbered) copies available. I don't know if they are 1/1 copies or not.

The Art of Dreamworks Animation

There is no Sanderson fiction in this book. A long time ago, Dreamworks licensed the Alcatraz series for an animated movie, and apparently got into the art phase of development. The movie was never greenlit, however, and no art was ever publicly released. Until this book. On page 309, in the middle of a section about the movie Home, there is a random piece of art filled with crazy road signs that contradict each-other. If you look closely at the signs at the top of the page, you can make out the word "ALCATRAZ", and in the lower left of the page, on what appears to be a train platform, the words "VERSUS THE EVIL LIBRARIANS" are hidden. Sanderson has confirmed that this is art from the movie that was never made for his books.

US Hardcover

ISBN	9781419711664
Release Year	2014
Publisher	Abrams
Cover Price	N/A
Cover Artist	Rhion Magee & Jeremiah Schaeffer
Estimated Value	$90

Out of print when I bought my copy, but appears to be back in stock on Amazon and other sites.

Australian Hardcover

ISBN	9781419745676
Release Year	2014
Publisher	Abrams
Cover Price	29.99 USD / 38 CAN
Cover Artist	Rhion Magee & Jeremiah Schaeffer

| Estimated Value | $90 |

When I originally found these books, this one was in print and readily available. It no longer seems to be available, and there was only one copy on eBay.

This edition says "national museum australia" on the spine.

The Wheel of Time

The first books that Sanderson ever co-wrote, and still the only co-writing that is majority Sanderson. These are the books that catapulted Sanderson to more mainstream fame in the fantasy community, because they were already so insanely popular. Sanderson's fame can be split into three eras (at least before an adaptation happens), with the secret projects Kickstarter beginning the third era, and *The Wheel of Time* kicking off the second.

All of these books come with a massive warning when buying online: 99% of the copies marketed as signed are NOT. All copies of all three of these books include a facsimile of Robert Jordan's signature, because Sanderson did not feel comfortable signing the books without that. Truly Sanderson-signed copies are decently rare and collectible, but the base hardcovers are very common.

Unlike almost all of the Jordan books, Tor did *not* print ARCs for any of the Sanderson books.

The Gathering Storm

Sanderson notoriously had trouble getting Mat right in this book, but it's still very good.

Leatherbound

ISBN	9780765302304
Release Year	2009
Publisher	Tor Books
Cover Price	N/A
Cover Artist	N/A
Estimated Value	$1600

There were 100 numbered and 26 lettered copies of this made. The estimated value is the price I was outbid at on a recent auction. If you know of any copies that are for sale for this price or less, please let me know!

US Hardcover

ISBN	9780765302304
Release Year	2009
Publisher	Tor Books
Cover Price	29.99 USD / 38 CAN
Cover Artist	Darrell K. Sweet
Estimated Value	$30

I regularly see these in my local used bookstore and on eBay for at or under cover price.

UK Hardcover

ISBN	9781841491653
Release Year	2009
Publisher	Orbit
Cover Price	20.00 GBP
Cover Artist	Larry Rostant and Lee Gibbons
Estimated Value	$30

Also fairly easy to find.

Towers of Midnight

This is it. This is the book that got me hooked on Sanderson's writing. This wasn't my first book, obviously, but it was the most compelling I had read so far, and it's the reason I went to read the rest of his stuff. Some of the foreshadowing in the earlier books starts to pay off here with some very satisfying conclusions and reveals.

Leatherbound

ISBN	9780765325945
Release Year	2010
Publisher	Tor Books
Cover Price	N/A
Cover Artist	N/A
Estimated Value	$1200

Estimated value is the purchase price of the copy I just got off of eBay. There are 151 copies, 125 numbered and 26 lettered.

US Hardcover

ISBN	9780765325945

Release Year	2010
Publisher	Tor Books
Cover Price	29.99 USD / 34.5 CAN
Cover Artist	Darrell K. Sweet
Estimated Value	$30

I regularly see these in my local used bookstore and on eBay for at or under cover price.

Note that there is a later printing of this hardcover (but not any of the other *Wheel of Time* books?) that is printed on thinner paper, and is significantly thinner on the shelf. This only really matters if you're hunting a true 1/1 or getting the Juniper dust jackets for the series (they have an option for either version).

UK Hardcover

ISBN	9781841498676
Release Year	2010
Publisher	Orbit
Cover Price	20.00 GBP
Cover Artist	Lee Gibbons
Estimated Value	$30

Also fairly easy to find.

A Memory of Light

This was originally supposed to be the title of the single final volume that Sanderson wrote, but after that was split into three books, the title was retained for the final final volume. Original cover art was supposed to be by Darryl K. Sweet, who did the covers for the other fourteen *Wheel of Time* books, but he passed away before finishing the art. You can still see his original (spoilery) draft online.

Leatherbound

ISBN	9780765325952
Release Year	2013
Publisher	Tor Books
Cover Price	N/A
Cover Artist	Michael Whelan
Estimated Value	$1200+

Limited to 26 lettered and 125 numbered copies. There is usually not much significant difference in price between the lettered and numbered copies, and there is no physical difference outside of the letter/number written in the book.

US Hardcover

ISBN	9780765325952
Release Year	2013
Publisher	Tor Books
Cover Price	34.99 USD / 39.99 CAN
Cover Artist	Michael Whelan
Estimated Value	$30

I regularly see these in my local used bookstore and on eBay for at or under cover price.

Fun fact: This is the first Sanderson hardcover that I got when I was fully caught up with his works and a massive fan, and could afford my own books. I went to Barnes and Noble on the day of release to buy my copy.

UK Hardcover

ISBN	9781841498720
Release Year	2012
Publisher	Orbit
Cover Price	25.00 GBP
Cover Artist	Lee Gibbons
Estimated Value	$30

Also fairly easy to find.

River of Souls

This story has only ever appeared in the Unfettered anthology (volume 1). It consists of scenes cut from *A Memory of Light* that give a little backstory to a character who shows up completely unexpectedly in that book with an army. The story is considered not strictly canon, but very close to it.

"ARC"

ISBN	9780984713639
Release Year	2013
Publisher	Grim Oak Press
Cover Price	30 USD
Cover Artist	Todd Lockwood

| Estimated Value | $300 |

Like all the Grim Oak hardcover "ARC"s, not a true ARC. It was sold on the website, not sent out for early reviews, and features the cover art, but in white. 250 copies were made.

Phoenix Comic Con Exclusive

ISBN	9780984713660
Release Year	2013
Publisher	Grim Oak Press
Cover Price	25 USD
Cover Artist	Todd Lockwood
Estimated Value	$1000

Limited to 250 copies, and only sold at that convention, this and the leatherbound of Unfettered are some of the rarest Grim Oak collectibles, not just from their Sanderson stuff. I have not seen any sales of this in recent years, so the value is purely guesswork. Your best bet for finding this or any other rare Grim Oak title will probably be their buy/sell/trade Facebook page.

Hardcover

ISBN	9780984713639
Release Year	2013
Publisher	Grim Oak Press
Cover Price	35 USD
Cover Artist	Todd Lockwood
Estimated Value	$100

There are two other editions to be aware of here. There is a second edition of the original hardcover, which shares the same ISBN, that has green cover art instead of the original purple. The copyright page on the green one even states it's a second edition, despite the same ISBN. And there is a 10th anniversary hardcover, ISBN 9781956000467, that has the original cover art but also a 10th anniversary emblem on the cover. Neither of the others are terribly collectible/rare.

Signed Limited Hardcover

ISBN	9780984713639
Release Year	2013
Publisher	Grim Oak Press
Cover Price	150 USD

| Cover Artist | Todd Lockwood |
| Estimated Value | $2000+ |

One of the top 10 most valuable Sanderson books. There were 500 numbered copies, and they are all signed to a tip-in page by every author in the collection, including Pat Rothfuss. Demand for these is super high because the others authors are collectible too. The books are leatherbound and wrapped in a pretty pink full-art dust jacket, and come with a slipcase. It has deckled edges.

Note that while 500 numbered copies were produced/sold, Grim Oak actually had the authors sign 600 pages, and the remaining 100 were turned into the unnumbered edition below.

Signed Unnumbered "Proof" Hardcover

ISBN	9780984713639
Release Year	2013
Publisher	Grim Oak Press
Cover Price	200 USD
Cover Artist	Todd Lockwood
Estimated Value	$2000+

See the note above about why 100 of these exist. I do not personally have a copy (let me know if you're selling one!). It has the same ISBN as the numbered hardcover, with the same full-art dust jacket. The book itself is cloth-bound, however, instead of the leather on the numbered edition, and comes without a slipcase. It has the same deckled edges as the numbered edition.

On the signature page, instead of a number, there is a big stamp of a key over the entire section where the number went on the numbered editions.

A Fire Within the Ways

This story has only ever appeared in the *Unfettered III* anthology. It is a deleted sequence from *A Memory of Light* that shows the cleansing of the Ways, but the timeline didn't fit with the book. Sanderson has stated that, while non-canon, something similar to the events of this story did happen after the end of *A Memory of Light*.

ARC

ISBN	9781944145231
Release Year	2019
Publisher	Grim Oak Press

Cover Price	N/A
Cover Artist	Todd Lockwood
Estimated Value	$50

This is a true ARC for the book, trade paperback and released before the actual book, sent to reviewers to generate publicity hype. However, a lot were made, and they have popped up fairly regularly on eBay. It is not hard to find. A quick search while writing turned up two copies for sale for under $100.

"ARC"

ISBN	9781944145231
Release Year	2019
Publisher	Grim Oak Press
Cover Price	50 USD
Cover Artist	Todd Lockwood
Estimated Value	$200

On the other hand, this is a fake ARC in the style of all the others, hardcover with white cover art, and sold directly on the Grim Oak website. There were only 250 copies made, but demand is not super high, and copies can readily be found online at the time of writing.

Hardcover

ISBN	9781944145231
Release Year	2019
Publisher	Grim Oak Press
Cover Price	30 USD
Cover Artist	Todd Lockwood
Estimated Value	$60

Out of stock/print, and slowly going up in price.

Emerald City Comic Con Exclusive

ISBN	9781944145347
Release Year	2019
Publisher	Grim Oak Press
Cover Price	50 USD
Cover Artist	Todd Lockwood
Estimated Value	$100

Limited to 250 copies, and originally supposed to be an exclusive to the convention. Extra copies were put up for sale on the Grim Oak website after they did not sell out at the con, and at some point the price was dropped to $30 as well. They are sold out now, however, and prices are rising.

Signed Limited Hardcover

ISBN	9781944145231
Release Year	2022
Publisher	Grim Oak Press
Cover Price	225 USD
Cover Artist	Todd Lockwood
Estimated Value	$225

Signed by all authors on two tip-in pages (the pages were split to speed up the signing process), and limited to 500 copies. Numbered copies were still available on the Grim Oak website at the time of writing.

The Rithmatist

Fans request sequels to this book more than any other non-Cosmere title, but Sanderson has been putting us off for ages. For now, the series consists of only a single book.

The Rithmatist

One of my favorite magic systems Sanderson has created. It's based around mathematics and chalk drawings, with circles and inscribed lines for defense. It would make for an absolutely amazing mobile game too.

ARC

ISBN	9780765320322
Release Year	2013
Publisher	Tor Books
Cover Price	N/A
Cover Artist	Christopher Gibbs
Estimated Value	$200

Not as common or cheap as Steelheart, but it's still a YA series that is less sought-after, and had a relatively high number of ARCs. They're not super common, but also not super rare.

US Hardcover

ISBN	9780765320322
Release Year	2013
Publisher	Tor Books
Cover Price	17.99 USD / 19.99 CAN
Cover Artist	Christopher Gibbs
Estimated Value	$25

A bit of patience and messaging sellers for pictures of the copyright page will find you one of these online pretty quickly.

The Reckoners

A completed YA trilogy that see humanity gaining super-powers, except everyone who gets the powers turns evil. Now a band of heroes known as the Reckoners are fighting back.

Steelheart

The first book in the series is focused completely around Chicago. It was on the tour for this book that I first met Sanderson, back in 2013!

US ABM

EAN	5800055049413
Release Year	2011-2012
Publisher	Peter Ahlstrom
Cover Price	N/A
Cover Artist	N/A
Estimated Value	$1000+

These copies were print-on-demand printed up by Peter in-house for Dragonsteel as promotional items. They are black paperbacks with no cover art. The "ISBN" isn't an ISBN, but simply an EAN for the book. Only 45 copies were printed (confirmed by Peter), and they are very rare. If you have a lead on one that is not personalized, please let me know!

US ARC

ISBN	9780385743563
Release Year	2013
Publisher	Delacorte Press
Cover Price	N/A

Cover Artist	Mike Bryan
Estimated Value	$100

YA, non-Cosmere, and a lot were printed. This is probably the easiest Sanderson-only ARC to obtain, and a great start to any ARC collection.

UK ABM

ISBN	N/A
Release Year	2013
Publisher	Gollancz
Cover Price	N/A
Cover Artist	N/A
Estimated Value	$1200+

We have no idea how many of these were made. Smaller trade paperback, with a white cover and no cover art. Only one copy is known among the collector community. If you have a lead on any copies, please let me know!

UK ARC

ISBN	9780575103856
Release Year	2013
Publisher	Gollancz
Cover Price	20.00 GBP / 12.99 GBP
Cover Artist	Sam Green
Estimated Value	$1000

Only one of these is known among the Collectors Guild, so we have no idea how many were actually made, and it's quite rare.

US Hardcover

ISBN	9780385743563
Release Year	2013
Publisher	Delacorte Press
Cover Price	18.99 USD / 21 CAN
Cover Artist	Mike Bryan
Estimated Value	$25

Note that this hardcover comes in two states. The true first state has a grey cover, with art by Mike Bryan. The second state has a blue cover with art by Craig Shields, who did the US cover art for the rest of the trilogy. The publisher changed the cover when the paperback of this book was released, and they took the unsold copies of the hardcover, which were still first printings, and replaced the dust jackets with the new ones. Only the first state with the grey cover is considered collectible. All of the exclusive editions below only exist in the grey cover.

US Hardcover Target Exclusive

ISBN	9780385743563
Release Year	2013
Publisher	Delacorte Press
Cover Price	18.99 USD / 21 CAN
Cover Artist	Mike Bryan
Estimated Value	$75

Has an Epic file in the back for Newton.

US Hardcover Walmart Exclusive

ISBN	9780385383714
Release Year	2013
Publisher	Delacorte Press
Cover Price	18.99 USD / 21 CAN
Cover Artist	Mike Bryan
Estimated Value	$75

The only one of the special editions to get a separate ISBN, for unknown reasons. Has an Epic file in the back for Obliteration.

US Hardcover Booksamillion Exclusive

ISBN	9780385743563
Release Year	2013
Publisher	Delacorte Press
Cover Price	18.99 USD / 21 CAN
Cover Artist	Mike Bryan
Estimated Value	$100

Seemingly the most difficult of the exclusive editions to find. Has an Epic file for Regalia in the back.

US Hardcover Barnes and Noble Exclusive

ISBN	9780385743563
Release Year	2013
Publisher	Delacorte Press

Cover Price	18.99 USD / 21 CAN
Cover Artist	Mike Bryan
Estimated Value	$60

Definitely the most common and easiest to find of the exclusive editions. Has an annotated version of the first chapter in the back, with Sanderson's commentary.

UK Hardcover

ISBN	9780575103856
Release Year	2013
Publisher	Gollancz
Cover Price	20.00 GBP
Cover Artist	Sam Green
Estimated Value	$60

Due to this being one of the first Sanderson UK hardcovers and having a low print run, this is decently more expensive than the US hardcover, though not crazily so.

Anderida Books also did a signed tip-in set, numbered and limited to 100 copies. These will typically run you $200+.

Mitosis

Originally a short story released as an e-book to promote Firefight. Features an Epic coming to Chicago who can split himself into clones. A UK hardcover came not much later, and we soon got a comic book as well.

Comic Book

ISBN	N/A
Release Year	2016
Publisher	Delacorte Press
Cover Price	N/A
Cover Artist	Ben McSweeney
Estimated Value	$75

While Ben did the art, the script is by Rik Hoskin, who later also wrote the script for the White Sand graphic novels.

While not very sought-after, this one is also fairly rare. Copies aren't usually super expensive, but also only appear for sale a few times a year.

UK Hardcover

ISBN	9781473209350

Release Year	2014
Publisher	Gollancz
Cover Price	8.99 GBP
Cover Artist	Sam Green
Estimated Value	$25

Super low demand is the main cause of the low price here.

Firefight

The middle book in the trilogy. This one moves the focus to Babylon Restored, which used to be New York City. The potato in a minefield line is one of my favorites in all of Sanderson's works.

ARC

ISBN	9780385743587
Release Year	2015
Publisher	Delacorte Press
Cover Price	N/A
Cover Artist	Craig Shields
Estimated Value	$250

This was, I believe, the first Sanderson ARC I ever owned. I won it in a Facebook contest that Sanderson hosted on his page, for who could get the most likes on their sharing of his post about this book coming out. I won first place, and received my ARC. It is still one of my most treasured ARCs, despite being one of the cheaper and easier to find ones.

US Hardcover

ISBN	9780385743587
Release Year	2015
Publisher	Delacorte Press
Cover Price	18.99 USD / 21.99 CAN
Cover Artist	Craig Shields
Estimated Value	$30

Not hard to find at all.

UK Hardcover

ISBN	9780575104211
Release Year	2015
Publisher	Gollancz

Cover Price	16.99 GBP
Cover Artist	Sam Green
Estimated Value	$50

Slightly harder to find than the US hardcover.

Anderida Books did a signed tip-in numbered set limited to 100.

Calamity

Calamity did not have any official ARCs. I have a semi-bound manuscript that I talk about in a later section of the book, but there are no official ARCs of this one.

US Hardcover

ISBN	9780385743600
Release Year	2016
Publisher	Delacorte Press
Cover Price	18.99 USD / 24.99 CAN
Cover Artist	Craig Shields
Estimated Value	$20

I feel like I see one of these at least once a month while hunting at used bookstores.

UK Hardcover

ISBN	9780575104662
Release Year	2016
Publisher	Gollancz
Cover Price	16.99 GBP
Cover Artist	Sam Green
Estimated Value	$45

Anderida Books did a signed, numbered tip-in set limited to 100.

Lux

An audio-original, this book does not exist in paper form.

The Cytoverse

Sanderson's latest YA universe, and likely to be his biggest, as Janci Patterson is still actively writing more books, and Sanderson has stated his intention to return as well in the future with more books.

Defending Elysium

This story was originally published in Asimov's Science Fiction magazine. Sanderson later decided to integrate it into the Cytoverse while writing Skyward. Not currently in print in English, but a prime candidate for the non-Cosmere anthology that Sanderson has recently announced.

Asimov's Science Fiction, October/November 2008 Issue

EAN	074470086215
Release Year	2008
Publisher	Dell Magazines
Cover Price	7.99 USD
Cover Artist	Virgil Finlay
Estimated Value	$50

Note that the barcode number is an EAN and not an ISBN here.

The challenge here isn't always finding the magazine, but finding one in good enough condition. Magazines are typically easier to damage than regular books, and are shipped unprotected in the mail. Plus, many people don't take care of them as carefully as they do their books.

Defending Elysium/Firstborn Con Double

ISBN	9781938570001
Release Year	2013
Publisher	Dragonsteel
Cover Price	17.99 USD / 18.99 CAN
Cover Artist	Dragos Jieanu / Donato Giancola
Estimated Value	$500

The first con double released by Dragonsteel. The Firstborn cover art is by Donato, the Defending Elysium cover art is by Dragos. This one is quite hard to find.

Skyward

Often subtitled "Claim the Stars". For many people, this is their favorite book in the series.

ARC

| ISBN | 9780399555770 |
| Release Year | 2018 |

Publisher	Delacorte Press
Cover Price	N/A
Cover Artist	Charlie Bowater
Estimated Value	$250

One of the easier ARCs to find, being non-Cosmere. We also suspect that Delacorte printed a lot of these, as it's the first book in a new series by a very popular author.

US Hardcover

ISBN	9780399555770
Release Year	2018
Publisher	Delacorte Press
Cover Price	19.99 USD / 25.99 CAN
Cover Artist	Charlie Bowater
Estimated Value	$40

The biggest thing to look out for on this one is a remainder mark. I see these with the remainder mark regularly at my local used bookstores.

UK Hardcover

ISBN	9781473217850
Release Year	2018
Publisher	Gollancz
Cover Price	18.99 GBP
Cover Artist	Sam Green
Estimated Value	$75

Beware of the second edition of the UK Hardcover, as that also has a first printing. The second edition is longer, including transcripts of some interview questions with Sanderson, and has the ISBN 9781473233249, but is not the true first and is less collectible.

Bulgarian Hardcover

ISBN	9786191931477
Release Year	2019
Publisher	Artline Studios
Cover Price	N/A
Cover Artist	Георги Мерамджиев (Georgi Meramdxhiev)
Estimated Value	$100

Hardcover sells this way short. The stylized ship on the front is raised wood against the wood boards that already make up the cover. Unfortunately, Artline Studios no longer ships directly to the US.

Starsight

Many people criticize this second book for taking us to a completely new location and starting with a new cast of characters. I personally don't mind, as this is the book where we get to meet Hesho and the other kitsen.

ARC

ISBN	9780399555817
Release Year	2019
Publisher	Delacorte Press
Cover Price	N/A
Cover Artist	Charlie Bowater
Estimated Value	$250

Later books in this series definitely had fewer ARCs than Skyward.

If you get your hands on an ARC, check it to see what Alanik was almost called. Make sure you say it out loud to get how bad it was.

US Hardcover

ISBN	9780399555817
Release Year	2019
Publisher	Delacorte Press
Cover Price	19.99 USD / 25.99 CAN
Cover Artist	Charlie Bowater
Estimated Value	$30

Super easy to find, but like Skyward, be on the lookout for remainder marks, as those seem to be fairly common on these.

UK Hardcover

ISBN	9781473217898
Release Year	2019
Publisher	Gollancz
Cover Price	20 GBP
Cover Artist	Sam Green
Estimated Value	$50

Bulgarian Hardcover

ISBN	9786191931941
Release Year	2020
Publisher	Artline Studios
Cover Price	N/A
Cover Artist	Георги Мерамджиев (Georgi Meramdxhiev)
Estimated Value	$100

Hardcover sells this way short. The stylized ship on the front is raised wood against the wood boards that already make up the cover. Unfortunately, Artline Studios no longer ships directly to the US.

Cytonic

There was no ARC for this third installment in the series. There was a US hardcover and UK hardcover, and as usual I included the Bulgarian hardcover for sheer awesomeness.

There is some debate on which order to put *Cytonic* and *Skyward Flight*. Here I've opted for the publication order of the physical hardcover books, which puts *Cytonic* first.

US Hardcover

ISBN	9780399555855
Release Year	2021
Publisher	Delacorte Press
Cover Price	19.99 USD
Cover Artist	Charlie Bowater
Estimated Value	$20

Trivial to find.

UK Hardcover

ISBN	9781473217935
Release Year	2021
Publisher	Gollancz
Cover Price	20.00 GBP
Cover Artist	Sam Green
Estimated Value	$40

Bulgarian Hardcover

ISBN	9786191932450
Release Year	2021
Publisher	Artline Studios
Cover Price	N/A
Cover Artist	Георги Мерамджиев (Georgi Meramdxhiev)
Estimated Value	$100

Hardcover sells this way short. The stylized ship on the front is raised wood against the wood boards that already make up the cover. Unfortunately, Artline Studios no longer ships directly to the US.

Skyward Flight

Cowritten by Janci Patterson, technically this is three separate stories/books: Sunreach, ReDawn, and Evershore. However, they have never been released as separate physical books in English. The one language that has done so is Dutch (Netherlands). There were no ARCs of any of these. Bulgaria has not done an edition of this one yet, unfortunately, so we just have the US and UK hardcovers.

US Hardcover

ISBN	9780593597852
Release Year	2022
Publisher	Delacorte Press
Cover Price	22.99 USD / 29.99 CAN
Cover Artist	Charlie Bowater
Estimated Value	$20

Numbered release copies were signed by both Sanderson and Patterson.

UK Hardcover

ISBN	9781399602136
Release Year	2022
Publisher	Gollancz
Cover Price	22.00 GBP
Cover Artist	Sam Green
Estimated Value	$30

Defiant

Despite skipping Cytonic/Skyward Flight, Delacorte did an ARC for this one. Bulgaria also has done an awesome hardcover. Additionally, Barnes and Noble did an alternate cover art edition.

ARC

ISBN	9780593309711
Release Year	2023
Publisher	Delacorte Press
Cover Price	N/A
Cover Artist	Charlie Bowater
Estimated Value	$300

These have been notoriously hard to find and acquire. Delacorte likely did a very small printing for the ARCs, being a later book in a series.

US Hardcover

ISBN	9780593309711
Release Year	2023
Publisher	Delacorte Press
Cover Price	21.99 USD
Cover Artist	Charlie Bowater
Estimated Value	$22

US Hardcover Barnes and Noble Edition

ISBN	9780593807651
Release Year	2023
Publisher	Delacorte Press
Cover Price	21.99 USD
Cover Artist	Charlie Bowater
Estimated Value	$25

The alternate cover art is the same as the original, just with a green background instead of an orange one. While there was not a signed edition for this one, Sanderson did sign a bunch of copies at the Barnes and Noble store at Dragonsteel Con in 2023.

UK Hardcover

ISBN	9781473234604
Release Year	2023

Publisher	Gollancz
Cover Price	25 GBP
Cover Artist	Sam Green
Estimated Value	$35

Bulgarian Hardcover

ISBN	9786191933594
Release Year	2024
Publisher	Artline Studios
Cover Price	N/A
Cover Artist	Георги Мерамджиев (Georgi Meramdxhiev)
Estimated Value	$100

Hardcover sells this way short. The stylized ship on the front is raised wood against the wood boards that already make up the cover. Unfortunately, Artline Studios no longer ships directly to the US.

Hyperthief

This story, written mostly by Janci Patterson, was originally released as the reward for the convention game at Dragonsteel 2023. Upon completing each part of the game, you received one piece of origami paper, with a chapter of the story printed on it. On the second day of the convention, the Dragonsteel store sold copies of the story as a little booklet, along with blank copies of the origami paper for folding copies of the various ships.

Remaining copies of the booklet were sold on the Dragonsteel website after the convention, and sold out quickly. Dragonsteel has stated they have no intention of restocking the book. Both versions have become collectible in well under a year.

Origami

ISBN	N/A
Release Year	2023
Publisher	Dragonsteel
Cover Price	N/A
Cover Artist	N/A
Estimated Value	$30

See notes above.

Booklet

ISBN	N/A
Release Year	2023
Publisher	Dragonsteel
Cover Price	N/A
Cover Artist	Anna Earley
Estimated Value	$50

See notes above.

Legion

The story of a guy who is *totally* not insane, and the adventures he has with the people who live inside his head. There are three main novellas in the sequence, as well as one additional story that is not written directly by Sanderson.

Legion

Fun fact: Moshe at the tomb is a tuckerization of Sanderson's editor, and the translator Kalyani is a tuckerization of a beta reader.

See also *Legion and The Emperor's Soul*, under *The Emperor's Soul* in the Cosmere/*Elantris* section.

ARC

ISBN	9781596064850
Release Year	2012
Publisher	Subterranean Press
Cover Price	N/A
Cover Artist	N/A
Estimated Value	$700

Quite rare. I only know of a handful of copies existing.

Blue cover paperback, with no cover art.

US Regular Hardcover

ISBN	9781596064850
Release Year	2012
Publisher	Subterranean Press
Cover Price	20.00 USD
Cover Artist	Jon Foster

Estimated Value	$50

While this has the same cover as the numbered edition, this one has blue cloth boards underneath.

US Numbered Hardcover

ISBN	9781596064850
Release Year	2012
Publisher	Subterranean Press
Cover Price	45.00 USD
Cover Artist	Jon Foster
Estimated Value	$200

Limited to 1,000 numbered copies, this edition is leatherbound.

US Dragonsteel Hardcover

ISBN	9781938570100
Release Year	2015
Publisher	Dragonsteel
Cover Price	15 USD
Cover Artist	Isaac Stewart
Estimated Value	$10

At the time of writing, Dragonsteel still had 169 copies of these for sale on their website, for $10 each. They are still first printings.

UK Hardcover

ISBN	9781473212633
Release Year	2013
Publisher	Gollancz
Cover Price	8.99 GBP
Cover Artist	Sam Green
Estimated Value	$25

Anderida did a numbered/signed tip-in set of 100 copies.

Legion: Skin Deep

The second story in the Legion series features one of Sanderson's best jokes (about Batman), a cameo by LSV, who is a famous M:tG player, and one of the most unfortunate title acronyms of any of his books: LSD.

ARC

ISBN	9781596066908

Release Year	2014
Publisher	Subterranean Press
Cover Price	N/A
Cover Artist	Jon Foster
Estimated Value	$750

Rare. This ARC has the cover art of the final book.

Other ARC

ISBN	9781596066908
Release Year	2014
Publisher	Subterranean Press
Cover Price	N/A
Cover Artist	N/A
Estimated Value	$750+

Blue cover that matches the Legion ARC. Equally rare, if not more so, than the Skin Deep ARC with cover art. Only one copy is known in the Collectors Guild, and I desperately want to acquire one. If you have a lead, please let me know.

US Numbered Hardcover

ISBN	9781596066908
Release Year	2014
Publisher	Subterranean Press
Cover Price	45 USD
Cover Artist	Jon Foster
Estimated Value	$150

2500 numbered copies were produced. Since the numbered copies for the first book in the series were limited to 1000, these have relatively low demand because fewer people get the first one and want to complete the set.

US Dragonsteel Hardcover

ISBN	9781938570117
Release Year	2015
Publisher	Dragonsteel
Cover Price	20 USD
Cover Artist	Isaac Stewart
Estimated Value	$10

At the time of writing, Dragonsteel still had 330 copies of these on sale on their website for $10 each. They are still first printings.

UK Hardcover

ISBN	9781473212497
Release Year	2015
Publisher	Gollancz
Cover Price	9.99 GBP
Cover Artist	Sam Green
Estimated Value	$20

Anderida Books did a signed, numbered tip-in set of 100 copies.

Legion: Lies of the Beholder

No ARCs were made for this story. However, Sub Press did realize Sanderson was a big deal, and did a lettered edition as well.

Additionally, rights to the series were sold to Tor to produce the Many Lives omnibus quickly enough that Dragonsteel did not produce an edition of this one, leaving their set as an unsatisfying pair.

US Lettered Hardcover

ISBN	9781596068858
Release Year	2018
Publisher	Subterranean Press
Cover Price	250 USD
Cover Artist	Jon Foster
Estimated Value	$500

Beware on listings when buying online, as this has the same ISBN as the numbered edition. Limited to 26 copies, though several PC copies have appeared as well.

US Numbered Hardcover

ISBN	9781596068858
Release Year	2018
Publisher	Subterranean Press
Cover Price	45 USD
Cover Artist	Jon Foster
Estimated Value	$75

Limited to 2500 numbered copies like Skin Deep. This one is the most readily available of the "trilogy", and I remember copies even being available on Amazon at one point.

UK Hardcover

ISBN	9781473224964
Release Year	2018
Publisher	Gollancz
Cover Price	12.99 GBP
Cover Artist	Sam Green
Estimated Value	$20

Anderida did their usual signed/numbered tip-in set of 100.

Legion: The Many Lives of Steven Leeds

This is simply a bind-up of the previous three stories in a single volume.

US Hardcover

ISBN	9781250297792
Release Year	2018
Publisher	Tor Books
Cover Price	27.99 USD / 36.5 CAN
Cover Artist	Miranda Meeks
Estimated Value	$30

The cover art on this one by Miranda is absolutely stunning.

UK Hardcover

ISBN	9781473225015
Release Year	2018
Publisher	Gollancz
Cover Price	16.99 GBP
Cover Artist	Sam Green
Estimated Value	$20

Anderida Books did a signed/numbered tip-in set of 150 copies.

Legion: Death and Faxes

No paper copies of this book exist, as it was an audio-original. I have only seen one CD copy of the audiobook, which I bought off eBay used from a library, in the same lot as the only CD copy of *Dark One: Forgotten* that I have ever seen.

Other - Fiction

Firstborn

This story was initially published in the Leading Edge magazine. Later, it was included in the *Firstborn/Defending Elysium* con double. Find that book under *Defending Elysium* in the Cytoverse. It was also in the even more rare Cardinalities anthology.

The story is available online for free for reading on Reactor Magazine, formerly known as tor.com.

Leading Edge Issue 50

Number	10495983
Release Year	2005
Publisher	Leading Edge
Cover Price	4.95 USD
Cover Artist	Daniel Hughes
Estimated Value	$50

Leading Edge is a magazine put out by the students at Brigham Young University (BYU), the school where Sanderson studied, as well as where he now teaches one creative writing class per year. It often features stories from the students at the school. While several issues of the magazine have small contributions from Sanderson, or simply list him as the editor, this one is notable for having the entire story of *Firstborn*. Available for many years on back order from BYU press, this magazine is now a bit more rare and is not trivial to find.

Note that the Number is something akin to an EAN here, and is definitely not an ISBN.

Cardinalities Hardcover

ISBN	N/A
Release Year	2014
Publisher	LTUE Press
Cover Price	N/A
Cover Artist	N/A
Estimated Value	$3000

This book had an incredibly limited hardcover run of only about 120 copies, and it's possible those 120 were split between the hardcover and the paperback. Only three copies have ever been acquired in the guild, making this one of the rarest books we know of.

The book was originally a fundraiser by the LTUE Press. LTUE (Life, The Universe, and Everything) is a local sci-fi/fantasy convention in Utah.

Cardinalities Paperback

ISBN	N/A
Release Year	2014
Publisher	LTUE Press
Cover Price	20 USD
Cover Artist	N/A
Estimated Value	$1000

More of these than the hardcover have been found, as the LTUE press had several copies left over in their office for a while, and by contacting them through their website you could buy one (or more) copies for the original price.

Features a slightly more purple cover than the hardcover, but again with no cover art.

Again, numbered out of 120, and it's possible those numbers are shared with the hardcover.

Snapshot

Initially released as a numbered and lettered edition by the short-lived Vault Books, this book was plagued with delays in release. It was later also released as part of the *Snapshot/Dreamer* con double.

This is rumored to be Sanderson's first book that will be made into a movie, so copies of this may see a spike in value if that happens.

Lettered Hardcover

ISBN	9780998559902
Release Year	2017
Publisher	Vault Books
Cover Price	250 USD
Cover Artist	Vincent Chong
Estimated Value	$700

This book was traycased, and limited to 78 copies (A-Z, AA-ZZ, AAA-ZZZ).

Numbered Hardcover

ISBN	9780998559902
Release Year	2017
Publisher	Vault Books
Cover Price	50 USD
Cover Artist	Vincent Chong
Estimated Value	$125

1000 numbered copies were produced. A copy just sold at auction on eBay for $122, on the day I was writing this.

Snapshot/Dreamer Con Double

ISBN	9781938570148
Release Year	2017
Publisher	Dragonsteel
Cover Price	20 USD
Cover Artist	Howard Lyon
Estimated Value	$50-75

The last of the con doubles. Still a bit of a rarity and commands a decent price.

Dreamer

This story, one of Sanderson's shortest, was originally published in the *Games Creatures Play* anthology. It was later reprinted in the *The Year's Best Dark Fantasy and Horror 2015* anthology, although that book is not considered collectible. There was no UK hardcover of *Games Creatures Play*, merely a paperback that I rarely see people collect.

It was also printed in the *Snapshot/Dreamer* con double that is listed right above this.

Games Creatures Play ARC

ISBN	9780425256879
Release Year	2014
Publisher	Ace Books
Cover Price	26.95 USD / 31.00 CAD
Cover Artist	N/A
Estimated Value	$1000

Green trade paperback with no cover art.

Games Creatures Play Hardcover

ISBN	9780425256879
Release Year	2014
Publisher	Ace Books
Cover Price	26.95 USD / 31 CAN
Cover Artist	Lisa Desimini
Estimated Value	$75

Many copies of this were printed, though we don't know exactly how many.

Perfect State

This story has never appeared on its own in English. You can find all of the joint publications under *Shadows for Silence in the Forests of Hell*, up in the Cosmere - Other Planets section.

A few foreign language editions have been published with this story, including the gorgeous Polish edition, but since it has several prior English editions, those editions are not considered collectible.

I Hate Dragons

Originally written by Sanderson as part of a writing exercise to tell an entire story with dialogue and no description, this story is available in its normal form and extended form for free on Sanderson's website. The only known publication in any language is in the Dragon Writers anthology. There is a paperback and a hardcover, but since most collectors want hardcovers whenever they are available, and we have no way of knowing which came first, I have only included the hardcover here.

US Hardcover

ISBN	9781680575156
Release Year	2016
Publisher	WordFire Press
Cover Price	N/A
Cover Artist	James A. Owen
Estimated Value	$27

Print-on-demand, with no actual number line to identify a first printing. These are readily available on Amazon and other online sites.

Infinity Blade: Awakening

Ah yes. THAT book. This book is notorious for being one of the most difficult Sanderson books to find, as you'll see from the prices below. Unfortunately, the e-book also disappeared from the internet when Chair Games ceased to exist, although at the time of writing the audiobook was still available on Audible. It is sometimes considered the "holy grail" of a complete hardcover Sanderson collection.

There are editions out in several foreign languages, and they are generally readily available.

The story is set in the universe of the Infinity Blade iOS games, and bridges the gap between the first and second games.

Hardcover

ISBN	9780983943013
Release Year	2012
Publisher	Chair
Cover Price	20 USD
Cover Artist	Adam Ford
Estimated Value	$2500+

Only 200 copies were produced, as far as we can tell, and many of these were numbered and signed at various conventions in 2012.

Paperback

ISBN	9780983943006
Release Year	2024
Publisher	Chair
Cover Price	N/A
Cover Artist	Adam Ford
Estimated Value	$2500+

Very little is known about the paperback other than that it is rarer than the hardcover. We suspect these may have been proof editions, internal for Chair and Sanderson, and never intended for a wide audience. Due to the small number of either book in existence, it commands an equally high price.

Infinity Blade: Redemption

While still rare, this book is considerably less so than *Awakening*.

The story is another part of the Infinity Blade universe, and is set between the second and third games in that series, and tells a much deeper story than *Awakening*. However, I doubt the stories make that much sense these days without watching the cutscenes from the games, as you won't know who some of the characters are. If you do wish to see those cutscenes, there are playthroughs and movies on YouTube.

Like *Awakening*, the e-book is gone, but the audiobook is still available on Audible.

Hardcover

ISBN	9780983943044
Release Year	2013
Publisher	Chair
Cover Price	20 USD
Cover Artist	Adam Ford
Estimated Value	$300

So much more common than *Awakening*, and often only sought by collectors who have found an *Awakening*, this book commands a much lower price, but is still quite rare. It was also sold at conventions, and later Sanderson's website.

Paperback

ISBN	9780983943037
Release Year	2014
Publisher	Chair
Cover Price	10 USD
Cover Artist	Adam Ford
Estimated Value	$200

Chair produced a number of these, maybe around 300, in preparation for a wider release. They were never sold publicly, despite being labeled for individual sale. Copies have been passed out from Sanderson's team after Chair went officially out of business, and I suspect they still have some in their warehouse.

Children of the Nameless

Freaking Wizards of the Coast. This story is Sanderson's affair with his long-time love: Magic: the Gathering (which is the best card game ever made). Wizards of the Coast, or WotC, who produce the game, allowed Sanderson to write a story in their universe, set on the plane of Innistrad. The story was initially released for free online, as Sanderson stipulated in his contract. WotC later broke that contract by taking the story off the internet, in preparation for a physical edition which they never published. There is no *legal* way to get a copy of this story in English now, something I desperately hope Sanderson and WotC get sorted out, as it's a really good story.

Various languages, including Spanish, German, Turkish, and Bulgarian, have published editions of this story, but you have to know those languages to be able to read them. I have left them out here because they are not considered collectible.

Fun fact: I brought my copy, which was a gift from fellow collector Chris McGrath (not the cover artist), of the Turkish edition of this book for Sanderson to sign, and he said it was the first copy of the book that he had ever signed, and so he numbered my copy #1. It is the only #1 copy I own, and to the best of my knowledge, the only numbered copy of *Children of the Nameless* to exist.

Dark One

Sanderson announced this universe with much fanfare a few years ago, saying it would be host to a plethora of multi-media stories and content. So far, we have only seen the first graphic novel in the series, and the audio-drama *Dark One: Forgotten*. Dan Wells is working on writing a novel set in this world as well. There was a Free Comic Book Day promo edition of the graphic novel, before the regular hardcover release, as well as two special editions that released at the same time.

Do not confuse Vault Comics, the publisher for this one, with Vault Books, who published *Snapshot*. They are completely unaffiliated companies.

Free Comic Book Day Promo

ISBN	859761006584
Release Year	2020
Publisher	Vault Comics
Cover Price	N/A
Cover Artist	Nathan Gooden
Estimated Value	$20

Originally given out for free at many comic book stores around the country, this has become mildly collectible but still shows up for sale regularly.

Hardcover

ISBN	9781939424761

Release Year	2020
Publisher	Vault Comics
Cover Price	N/A
Cover Artist	Nathan Gooden
Estimated Value	$35

The first batch of preorders of this book through Dragonsteel received a special signed Dark One bookplate. The bookplate is more collectible than the book itself at this point.

Bookstore Hardcover

ISBN	9781939424457
Release Year	2021
Publisher	Vault Comics
Cover Price	24.99 USD / 33.99 CAN
Cover Artist	Nathan Gooden
Estimated Value	$35

This edition was available through normal bookstores. I think the non-promo hardcover was available through online booksellers, such as Amazon, while this one was available through brick-and-mortar stores.

Barnes and Noble Hardcover

ISBN	9781939424679
Release Year	2021
Publisher	Vault Comics
Cover Price	24.99 USD / 33.99 CAN
Cover Artist	Nathan Gooden
Estimated Value	$30

This edition was, as the name might imply, available only through Barnes and Noble. It was sold on their website, however, and did not require you to visit a store in person. It came with two posters, one of the cover art for this edition, and one of the map.

Dark One: Forgotten

An audio-only book that actually makes sense as an audiobook. It's written by Dan Wells as a prelude to the Dark One universe, and follows a college student as she makes a podcast with her friend to talk about mysterious disappearances and unsolved murders. It is a very Dan Wells story, and it works perfectly as an audiobook.

There are no standard physical editions of this book. I have a CD copy that I got used from a library in the same lot as my copy of *Legion: Death and Faxes*, but I believe this is a copy that the library may have made for themselves.

The Original

Audio-only book with no physical form. It was written primarily by Mary Robinette Kowal. I have never even seen a CD of this one.

The Frugal Wizard's Handbook for Surviving Medieval England

The red-headed step child of Sanderson's record-breaking Kickstarter campaign, this hilarious time travel/memory loss romp through an alternate England was the only non-Cosmere story of the original secret projects. Numbered copies of this one have sold for considerably less than numbered copies of the other secret projects, and the book is generally considered to be the least desirable of them, despite being one of my favorite stories.

UK ARC

ISBN	N/A
Release Year	2023
Publisher	Gollancz
Cover Price	N/A
Cover Artist	N/A
Estimated Value	$700

Blue paperback, shorter than a typical ARC, with the cover art. Despite there only being one known copy, I am putting the value a little low here, because of the lack of demand I've seen for this one.

Dragonsteel Deluxe Edition

ISBN	9781938570339
Release Year	2023
Publisher	Dragonsteel
Cover Price	55 USD
Cover Artist	Steve Argyle
Estimated Value	$55

The only non-Cosmere, and therefore least popular of the secret projects, but still with a first print run of 150,000, this one is in stock on the

Dragonsteel store at the time of writing, and likely will remain there for quite a while.

US Tor Hardcover

ISBN	9781250899675
Release Year	2023
Publisher	Tor Books
Cover Price	29.99 USD
Cover Artist	N/A
Estimated Value	$30

Although hardcover printings have moved on, this is criminally easy to get.

UK hardcover

ISBN	9781399613408
Release Year	2023
Publisher	Gollancz
Cover Price	22 GBP
Cover Artist	N/A
Estimated Value	$30

Long Chills and Case Dough

Sanderson's surprise gift to us in the last of the Year of Sanderson boxes was this book, an old novella from when Sanderson was in college. It's a very interesting story, with an intentionally misogynistic main character. Copies are still plentifully available through the Dragonsteel store, and it is not considered rare. I am including it here for completeness sake.

Hardcover

ISBN	9781938570469
Release Year	2023
Publisher	Dragonsteel
Cover Price	12.00 USD
Cover Artist	Ben McSweeney
Estimated Value	$12

All art, including interior art, is by Ben McSweeney, although he is not directly credited.

There is an excellent audiobook version on YouTube for free, produced by Steve over on his RAFO (Read And Find Out) channel.

Other - Nonfiction

La Virtud de Divertir: En Defensa de la Literatura de Evasión

This was a speech that Sanderson delivered in 2006, as a just-published author with only Elantris out in the world. He delivered the speech at the UPC conference in Spain. I have been told that the event was more like an awards gala, like we would see for the Hugo Awards, than it was an actual conference. Regardless, Sanderson gave this speech, likely in English, and it was recorded and translated for the conference's publication. It is only available in Spanish.

XVI Premio UPC/Novela corta de ciencia ficción

ISBN	9788466632003
Release Year	2007
Publisher	Ediciones B
Cover Price	N/A
Cover Artist	Estudio Ediciones B
Estimated Value	$20

Sanderson's speech is pages 13-22. When I had him sign my copy of this book a few years ago, he said it was the first time he had ever been asked to sign that speech.

The cover is red and depicts what appears to be a water droplet hovering over a barren landscape.

This book is not to be confused with the XVII version, which was from the conference/awards the following year. That year, *Defending Elysium* won an award, and was printed in the book, though that book, which is blue, is generally not considered collectible because the Asimov's publication in the US came first. I still have a copy. Who do you think I am?

Writing Fantasy Heroes

This book includes a short essay by Sanderson about writing fight scenes. The essay is not available anywhere else, though all the advice he gives is available across his writing class and Writing Excuses episodes.

Paperback

ISBN	9780982053683
Release Year	2013

Publisher	Rogue Blades Entertainment
Cover Price	N/A
Cover Artist	Dleoblack
Estimated Value	$16

Despite having the little barcode in the back to indicate that this is print-on-demand, the book does have a full number line. It appears to still be readily in print.

There are Still Stories to Tell

Included in the Sanderson box (December 2023) from the Year of Sanderson, this is a notebook with a stack of writing prompts that Sanderson has accumulated as ideas over the years, with plenty of blank pages for you to write something based on those prompts.

Paperback

ISBN	N/A
Release Year	2023
Publisher	Dragonsteel
Cover Price	N/A
Cover Artist	N/A
Estimated Value	$10

Although this notebook has no cover art, the endpapers are by Randy Vargas.

Curso de Escritura Creativa

This book is only available in Spanish. It is a translation of a transcript of the publicly available videos of Sanderson's Creative Writing class for one semester, including student questions and answers. Upon release the book came with a blank notebook.

Paperback

ISBN	9788466671897
Release Year	2022
Publisher	Sine Qua Non
Cover Price	20.90 Euro
Cover Artist	Penguin Random House Grupo
Estimated Value	$20

This is the book itself.

Notebook

ISBN	N/A
Release Year	2022
Publisher	Sine Qua Non
Cover Price	N/A
Cover Artist	Penguin Random House Grupo
Estimated Value	$10

    This is a little casewrapped hardcover, with red sprayed page edges, a red ribbon bookmark, and a red elastic ribbon page holder in the back.

Sanderson Swag Guide by Murphy Thomas

Murph is an Australian Sanderson Collector, and the widely acknowledged master of everything Sanderson SWAG. I collect the books, he collects everything else (but also the books). His collection is amazing and visually stunning, and his knowledge of everything SWAG is encyclopedic. You can find videos of some of his collection on YouTube under "Brandon Sanderson SWAG and LOOT Archive". When I first conceptualized this book, I knew I wanted Murph to help with the SWAG chapter. He went above and beyond, writing the entire chapter himself and including some great pictures. Here it is:

SWAG "STUFF WE ALL GET"

Some book collectors love a clean shelf with nothing obstructing the perfection of a perfectly aligned and grouped collection of book spines. And then there are those slightly eccentric collectors with their busy shelves that must display everything that goes with the books. What goes on a shelf with a book other than another book you ask?

Let me introduce you to the incredible world of SWAG and why it's so special to many collectors.

What makes it special? SWAG can give an author another creative outlet to show a reader the world and the characters they created. This physical connection is often overlooked but it can be a powerful medium to attract a reader or give the reader something physical from the story they just read. Brandon's SWAG has been fantastic at giving his fans that physical connection and the art has been key to this. From the maps of his worlds, booklets and guides, oversize bookmarks, buttons or special handout pins, there is something beautiful that has been released with almost every book in his catalogue.

SWAG are those small inexpensive promotional goodies that most authors use to promote their books. They allow an author to show their appreciation to a reader that has purchased a book of theirs or often given out to attendees of an event that the author, publisher or bookstore has organised. The most common promotional items you will see are bookmarks, stickers and buttons but there are the exceptions and when it comes to Brandon Sanderson you will see why his SWAG is some of the best and in my opinion, the most amazing in the world of SWAG collecting.

Publishers are responsible for a lot of the SWAG but Brandon's team of artists and designers involved in its production since the very early days. The artistic/promotional team of InkWing was where it all started, and it has since evolved into what we now know as Dragonsteel with professionals heading up every department to ensure its brand and IP are maintained and fans are excited by the products.

How to get it?

This depends on how much you want it. The best way to get official SWAG is by attending one of Brandon's ticketed book release events held at Dragonsteel Nexus in Salt Lake City, USA. The events are ticketed and provide attendees with several levels of SWAG and merchandise. The SWAG and merchandise that accompany the event tickets are limited and are not usually available to buy after the event.

Some books do have SWAG available with in-store or online purchases, but these are becoming less common and often require you to email your details and proof of purchase to get the item on offer. Your other op-

154

tions are keeping an eye on Brandon's social media accounts. His team do travel to a few cons throughout the year and the Dragonsteel store may have a few goodies or special SWAG items made especially for that event. The Dragonsteel store is another potential source of SWAG. If you place an order, you may get lucky and find a sticker or two with your purchase.

Finding any SWAG is not as easy as you might think because most people don't value it, so it's not listed for sale. Try looking in the usual places like eBay, Mercari or Marketplace but your best bet for SWAG is in the Sanderson collector groups.

Rare SWAG Guide

SWAG that was given out in the early years is extremely hard to find. Its rarity comes down to several factors, subject matter, the amount made, size and material but people discarding SWAG after the novelty has worn off and not seeing value in the items is the real reason. Listed below are some of my favourite and most desirable SWAG/Collectibles that were available to purchase from Brandon's stores or free from an event promoting one of Brandon's books in the USA.

Mistborn Mini Figurines

Were available in display pewter, 'ready to paint' pewter with a primer or hand-painted version by Drew Olds. Sold individually or as a set. Heroic 28mm scale (ranging from 1" to 2" in height.) Drew Olds believes that the Koloss and Vin are the rarest with around 200 casts and around 300 casts of Kelsier and Inquisitor. The pewter figurines were the highest selling option.

Vin Assassin Token

Brandon Sanderson and artist Steve Argyle shared a booth at the 2017 Gen Con 50 and to celebrate they created the 2 individual Vin Tokens, and the quantities were split between them.

Several thousand Warrior Tokens were made but only a few hundred of the Assassin Token. To get one from Brandon you had to complete a MTG

Token scavenger hunt. According to Brandon's post about the event, all his Assassin tokens would be pre-signed.

Rithmatist Chalk Bag

The Rithmatist Chalk Bag is a felt finish drawstring pouch with silver foil lettering. It contained 2 x large yellow pieces of chalk in Ziplock bag and a detailed Rithmatist training booklet.

Szeth die-cut card with code

Brandon Sanderson and Tor Books, an imprint of Tom Doherty Associates, LLC teamed up to create more than 1,000 die-cut pop-out cards of Szeth "The Assassin in White". The die-cut cards include a code for fans to unlock secret goodies and giveaways on Brandon's website.

Brandon distributed the die-cut cards with signed bookplates inside copies of Words of Radiance during his USA release tour.

Complete set of 4 Firefight Punch Cards

There are a total of 4 cards in a set containing 3 character punch cards and 1 Firefight Book promo card. The character cards are of Newton, Obliteration and Regalia.

Non book collectibles

Dragonsteel is a powerhouse of creativity, and the quality and design of its merchandise is excellent. Brandon and his team have been offering merchandise on his store since around 2010. From Mistborn figurines and vials of metals to Jewelry and clothing, the Dragonsteel Store has been offering collectors and fans the opportunity to purchase collectibles from the stories they love. Although fans and collectors refer to non-book collectibles as SWAG it should be noted that the main difference is that collectibles are available to purchase and not usually limited to book release events or tours. Collectibles have been available to fans in many forms over the years and have been produced by individuals and companies holding a license to produce the products.

Foreign Edition SWAG

Foreign editions of Brandon's books occasionally have SWAG available at a book release or tour. The UK and Spain are the main countries outside of the USA to have produced SWAG and it is some of the rarest to collect. The products are mainly from Brandon's pre-

157

COVID international book release events but several pieces in recent years have been from publishers or independent bookstores.

Free Vs Purchased

As a loose rule, SWAG is free, but this rule is very loose. The trouble with SWAG is that it is often added to exclusive event ticket or book purchases. A good example of paying for SWAG are the VIP tickets available to purchase at Dragonsteel Nexus.

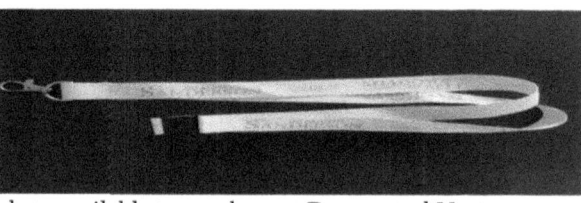

Crossover SWAG

The crossover SWAG and collectibles are out there and will most likely become more numerous as the years go by. Infinity Blade is my favourite because I like the game, and its collectibles are extremely rare. The Wheel of Time has a lot of amazing items to collect but they can be very difficult to find due to the age of the books.

Non-Licensed SWAG and Collectibles

The trouble with being a popular author is that it attracts interest from people trying to cash in on the Dragonsteel brand by making unlicensed merchandise. You will find a lot of it around on some internet sites but please avoid it. The Sanderson Collectors Guild is a wealth of knowledge and has members that can help advise you if you are unsure if the product is licensed.

The Value of SWAG and Collectibles

Values can be the most difficult part of collecting SWAG and collectibles. The newer items are mostly sold between collectors for advertised cost or traded, but the rare pieces are continually increasing in value due to more people enjoying SWAG collecting and its limited availability. A Unicorn piece like a complete set of Mistborn Pewter figurines painted by Drew Olds can see prices over several thousands of dollars, a *Stormlight Archive Pocket Companion* might see several hundred dollars and a Reckoners set of Calamity punch cards may see something under a hundred dollars. Many items are affordable to most collectors but as with all collectibles, value is driven by demand, supply, timing and who wants it more, so be prepared but above all, enjoy the hunt.

Unicorns and Curiosities in my Personal Collection

Over the years, I've acquired some things that I don't really consider official collectibles, because they are the only one that exists, and are typically not official products. These are the true heart of my collection, and I love every one of them to death. I will attempt to describe them here with as much detail as I can.

Mistborn Leatherbound Process books

This is a collection of several items that Dragonsteel got during the process of creating the *Mistborn* leatherbound books.

There is a paperback glued oversized copy of each of the 3 books. These copies are in full color, and show the pages with margins, as they will be cut for the book itself. They are not the actual paper that is used, instead being uniformly glossy.

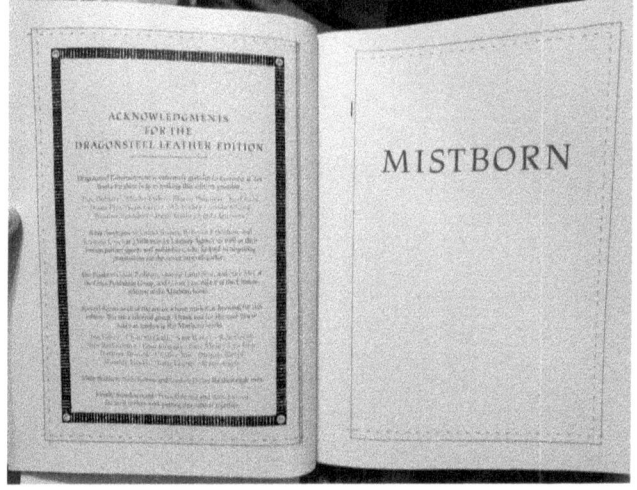

There is a set of unbound copies of each book. These are the book, with pages cut and folded into signatures, but before binding. You can see how the signatures are put together to form the final book, and you can see how the art pages are slotted in between the regular pages, with special paper.

There is a printed, bound paperback proof of The Hero of Ages, which is as close to an ARC/ABM as exists for the leatherbounds. It is the same size as the final book, although it is glued instead of sewn. It gives info about the printer on the front, and was produced as the final step in the printing/proofing process.

Calamity Beta Draft with my notes

Calamity was the first book that I beta read. I printed out the beta draft, and did the beta read from that. I hole-punched the entire thing and put it in a blue three-ring binder. My notes, which were converted to a spreadsheet later, are on loose paper at the end of the binder. I also scribbled occasional notes about grammar and whatnot on the book itself. My copy is signed by Sanderson, from his stop in Austin on the Calamity tour.

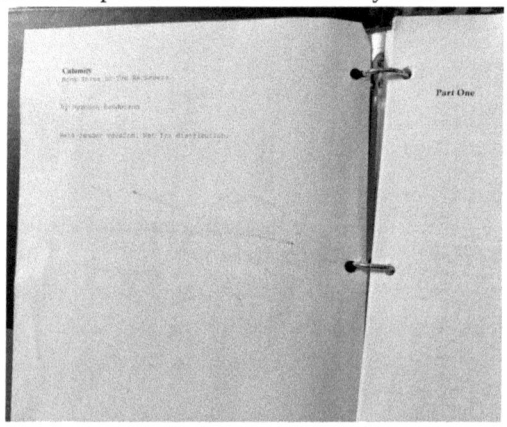

Calamity Advance Bound Thing

This is not a proper ARC. It's an A11 paper printing of a draft of the book with the final formatting, but is bound like you might see a thesis or something in college, with the pages glued together and clear plastic over the front instead of a cover. I received this from a friend who worked for a publisher at the time, and believe it to be an internal advance copy that was printed up causally and not an official ARC.

Skyward Flight Brainstorming Notes

These handwritten notes come to me as a gift from Janci Patterson. They are the original brainstorming notes, with ideas for Sunreach, ReDawn, and Evershore, some of which we can see in the final stories, and some of which never made it in. They were taken by Janci during her initial planning process, which involved several phone calls with Sanderson to hash out ideas for the series.

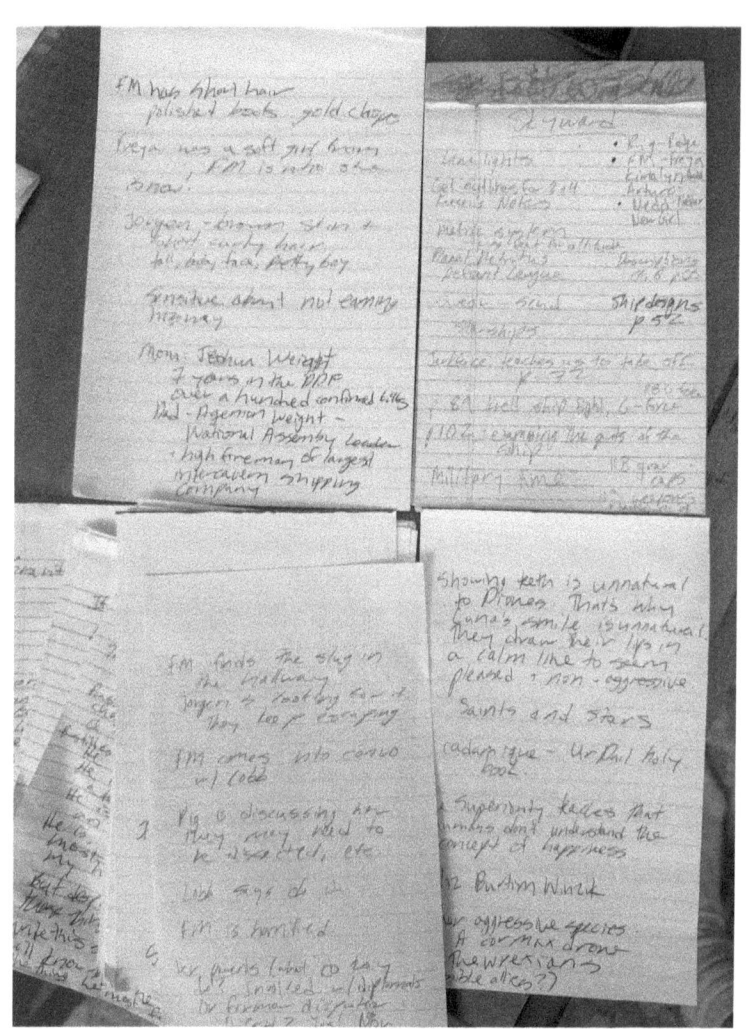

Handwritten Page from White Sand Prime

White Sand Prime was the first novel that Brandon wrote. He wrote it by hand in a notebook, largely while working the night shift at hotels. It has never been published. Several years ago, Brandon gifted me with a singular page from that notebook, written front and back. It features some spectacularly bad spelling/grammar/handwriting, and makes me very glad that Brandon has switched to typing up his manuscripts now. It is probably the most unique and valuable item in my collection.

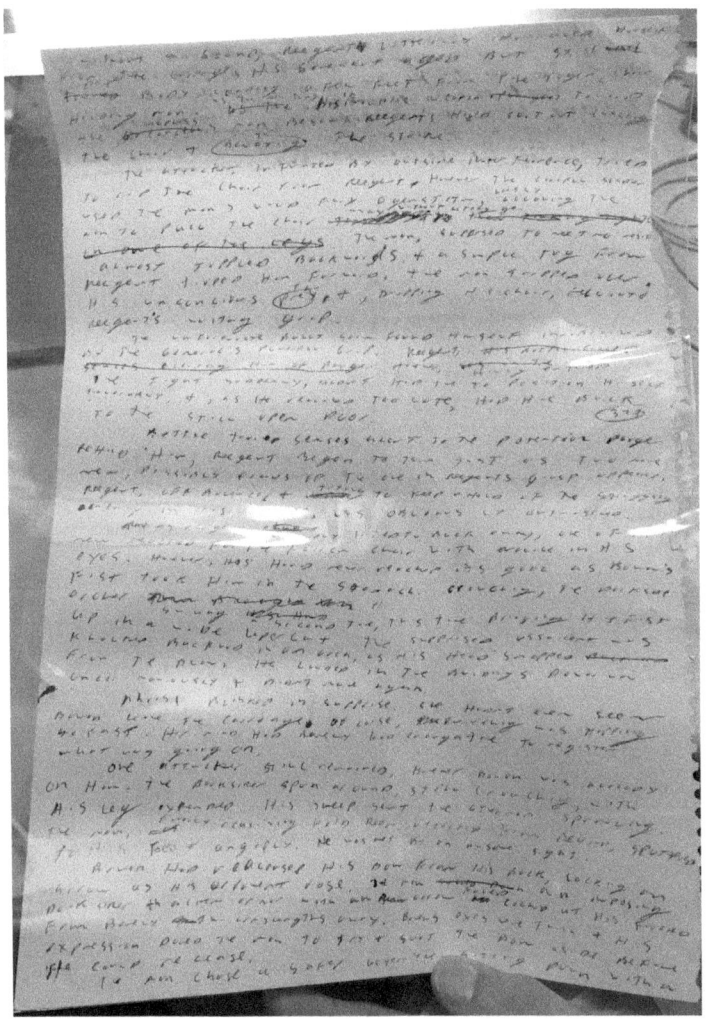

My Guestbook

Custom made for me by Reed (@FracturedPhalanx) from the SCG, this is not a Sanderson book. It is *my* book. It has my glyph on the outside and says "THE SANDERSON LIBRARY" "ZENEF MARK" on the spine. It is leatherbound. On the inside, it is a blank lined notebook. Whenever someone visits my library, I have them write a little note about visiting, and sign and date it. In addition, whenever someone sends me a book for my collection, I ask if they want to include a little note, which I tape into the guestbook.

If you want to see all of the books listed above, as well as a few hundred random paperbacks and foreign editions, and meet me in person, please drop me a line on Discord, Facebook Messenger, or Instagram, or at thesandersoncollector@gmail.com. I would love to have you come and sign my guestbook.

The first page of the guestbook is reserved for when Brandon himself visits my library.

Afterword and Acknowledgments

If you've made it this far in the book, thank you for reading! It's *you* who makes all of this possible. From the first dozen views on my first video ever to the entire SCG full of friends that I know today, y'all have let me know that you enjoy seeing and reading about my collection and that I should keep sharing my knowledge.

Above and beyond the general mass of friends that I have, there's a handful of people that I specifically want to acknowledge for their help with this book and my collecting journey.

The first person that I want to acknowledge is Kira. My partner since 2019, and the person who kept me sane through the pandemic. She has believed in me the entire time, pushing me to do better and be better in all aspects of my life, even on days when I want to give up on myself. When I decided earlier this year (2024) that I was going to write, edit, produce, and publish this book before DSNX in December, she didn't hesitate to tell me to do it and ask what I needed. She has been more than accommodating in making time for me to write, has been my first sounding board for many of my crazy ideas, and has been ceaselessly supportive of me. Thank you, Babe. I love you. Forever.

Brandon Sanderson didn't *directly* help with the writing of this book, but of course, none of this would exist without him and the stories he tells. Brandon, you're awesome (and you know it), and I hope you keep telling your stories for many years to come and giving me endless books to collect, until they all fall over and crush me to death.

Murphy Thomas wrote the entire SWAG chapter for this book, and was a sounding board for my crazy ideas before I even thought this book would be an actual thing. Thank you so much for helping out, and for all the awesome trades over the years.

Janci Patterson is amazing. I came to her at the absolute last minute to ask if she was interested in writing a foreword for me, and I am delighted and honored that she said yes. And I am eternally grateful for the kind and eloquent words she provided. Thank you so much!

Speaking of last-minute saves, I want to give a hearty thanks to my cover artist, Lotus (Siena). She shortened her usual turnaround time by an order of magnitude to get me this amazing art and design, and I hope y'all are as happy to have it on your shelves as I am.

This book would be a lot worse and harder to read without a team of beta/gamma readers who worked on insanely tight deadlines to give me loads of feedback and make this book so much better. They caught many errors and mistakes, and cleaned up a lot of my rather atrocious grammar. They were: Kevin F. Dush (Duck Dad), Ene Nytch, Luke DeProst, Edgar Brown, Nisarg Shah, Cameron Irwin (Papa Noff), Paige Vest, Kalyani Poluri, and Jimmy Conner, and every one of them was incredible.

The entirety of Dragonsteel Books is amazing too. They produce and ship many of the special editions and SWAG, and work tirelessly to make sure Brandon can spend as much time writing as possible, while us fans can get as many awesome things as possible. Thank you to all of you, even the Dougs (especially the Dougs)!

Isaac ſtewart is part of Dragonsteel, but he needs a special shout-out. He has been instrumental in helping me get some of the coolest parts of my collection, like the leatherbound process books and Star's End, but he also sat down with me some years ago and we worked together to design a personal glyph, which has meant so much to me (full story in the epilogue). And that's not to mention that he designs and creates all of the amazing special editions that Dragonsteel produces, creating or directing all of the art that goes into every single book. Thank you for all you do, Isaac, and thank you for being my friend.

Also at Dragonsteel, there is a person who is assigned to helping me with foreign language editions. It was initially Joe Deardeuff, then Christi, and now it's Jen. While I didn't include many translated editions in this book, those editions are a major part of my collection, and I cannot thank y'all enough for your help in this area.

Writing this book has been an amazing experience. So much of this knowledge lives in my head, or scattered across various videos and pictures and Discord channels. I'm so excited that I can bring it together in one place, and while I know that the primary audience for this book will be other collectors who want to use it as a reference or for some reading to brush up on terminology, it is my hope that someday, somewhere, a copy will find its way to a Sanderfan who may not have even considered collecting before, and it will inspire them to start their own exciting journey of Sanderson Collecting.

Epilogue: A Longer Biography of The Sanderson Collector

I have ADHD. I've had it my whole life, but wasn't diagnosed and medicated until the last few years. When I was a kid, I didn't really even know what ADHD was. I was homeschooled, and not on a lot of internet spaces, so I didn't get the mental health meme dumps that people seem to get these days.

What this did mean as a kid is that I was very undisciplined and unfocused, with a lot of energy. My poor mother (hi Mom!) enrolled me in martial arts when I was 6, and I did it for the next 12 years, or so.

At some point -- I don't remember exactly when -- I went to an international competition and trip for the style of martial arts that I practiced. It was in Korea, and it was a blast. On the trip, I met a girl who was also doing the martial arts competition, and developed a bit of a crush on her. So, of course, I wanted to do whatever I could to impress her.

On the plane flight home, we switched seats around so I could sit next to her. The person next to us was reading a book, and she got interested in the book. I wrote down the name of the book and decided to read it, as well as send the info to the girl.

I saw her a few more times after that, and we're still friends who chat occasionally, but the biggest life takeaway for me from that trip was the book. I went home, found the series it was a part of, and read it.

That book was *Knife of Dreams*.

I quickly became an avid fan of *The Wheel of Time* series, devouring all the books and rereading many of them. I was devastated when I reached the end of the series and learned that my beloved Robert Jordan had passed away.

When I found out that some upstart kid named Brandon Sanderson was taking over the series, I wanted to see if he was any good, and if his contributions would be worth reading. I got myself a copy of *Mistborn* and read it.

I admit that I wasn't immediately hooked. *Mistborn* was good, yes, but that book alone didn't blow my mind. I decided that Sanderson was a competent writer, and he could probably do good enough on the *Wheel of Time* series to be worth reading. I picked up the next couple books as they came out in paperback, and read them.

The Gathering Storm was solid. Not the same as a Robert Jordan book, but still pretty good. I enjoyed it, and looked forward to *Towers of Midnight*.

And that's where things really took off. In particular, there's one scene that involves a cup of tea, the color of a dress, and my favorite brown ajah character. If you've read the book, you probably know the one I'm talking about.

That scene. That bloody scene.

It was one of the most satisfying payoffs for subtle foreshadowing over the course of a series that I have ever read. I am tearing up now, writing this, from the emotional impact of that scene.

I was hooked. I knew that Brandon was paying off foreshadowing that Jordan had put in place years ago, but he delivered it so seamlessly and satisfyingly that I had to see if he could do it on his own. I bought the rest of the *Mistborn* trilogy and read them and... Yeah. Brandon can rusting do it. He is a storytelling genius. The end of *The Hero of Ages* absolutely devastated me, in the best way possible.

I very quickly devoured everything else that Brandon had written, going so far as to get *Armored* in order to read *HARRE*. Brandon was my favorite author, and there was no going back.

This was right as I was starting college and still living with my parents. When I was a kid, my parents very much promoted reading and books. My favorite days were the times about once a month we went out to Barnes and Noble or Borders (Rest in Peace) to get more books. My copies of *Redwall* were falling apart from being reread so many times. But the rule always was that we get books when they come out in paperback. Hardcovers are too expensive, and there's plenty of other books to read while you wait. Just be patient.

I distinctly remember that the point I caught up with Brandon's work was right after *The Alloy of Law* came out. It had a hardcover release, but not a paperback. I waited anxiously for it to come out, so that I could read the latest and greatest. I remember a friend I made taking the train to school teasing details about the new metals and time manipulation, and me being so, so eager to get my hands on it.

That was in 2012. By 2013, I was living in the dorms at college and working as a learning assistant. I had a tiny space, with barely enough room for a single shelf of books, so of course I brought my entire Sanderson collection with me. *Steelheart* came out in September 2013, and Brandon made a stop in my town on that tour. I bought a copy of the book in hardcover with my own money, and went to the event and met Brandon.

That event is still one of the best days of my life. I had two heavy bags full of Brandon's books, and this was before he was mega-popular. I came up to him in the hallway after a panel, because he said that he would be out there signing books if anyone wanted to come talk to him. I presented him with all my books, and he exclaimed that I must have everything. I noted that I was missing a few small things, such as *Infinity Blade: Awakening*, as it had only been sold at some other conventions.

Brandon, being storming wonderful like he is, and recognizing me as such an avid fan, told me to email his store director, Kara, and she would get me sorted out. She did, and has been my hero ever since.

I must have seemed slightly crazy with all the books I had and wanted to get signed. Brandon's handler at that event covertly asked him several times if he wanted to get away from me, because I was monopolizing his time. I was the last person in line, though, and he was happy to literally sit down on the floor and sign my books. That personal touch, something that's impossible to get these days, is what completely cemented who I am now.

Brandon was already my favorite author. *The Way of Kings* and *The Hero of Ages* were vying for the best book I had ever read. And after that day, that conversation with him and that little gift to a budding collector, he was one of my favorite people ever.

At that point, I was just determined to have a copy of everything Brandon had ever written. It wasn't until a year or two later that I was at my local Half-Price Books, when I found a used hardcover of *The Alloy of Law*, that I decided I wanted all the hardcovers. And since I already had the personalized paperbacks, I couldn't very well get rid of those, so I might as well have both. Brandon was essentially my religion at that point anyway. Things quickly devolved from there, and I started collecting the UK editions as well.

I was on book twitter before then as well, and it's there that I met Nikki, a fellow Sanderfan from Seattle. She did a giveaway of a Brandon book on her book blog (aptly named "There Were Books Involved") and Brandon retweeted the giveaway. I followed her from that tweet, and we soon became friends.

The two of us then started a twitter account called Sanderson Army. It was an absolute blast of a time running it with her. For a while, I would search twitter for Brandon's name, and like every tweet that came along, as well as respond to all the questions I could. I posted news about new book releases. Nikki posted awesome fanart. We became a known quantity in the fan community, and Peter, Brandon's assistant, followed us.

It was an absolute shock and delight when, a few years later, Peter privately messaged us on the Sanderson Army account asking if either or both of us wanted to be beta readers for *Calamity*.

Obviously, when I picked my jaw up off the floor I said yes. Nikki did as well.

Calamity wasn't actually the first released Sanderson work that I beta'd, though. Brandon wrote *Mistborn: Secret History* soon after, and released it on a very quick schedule, as an e-book only alongside the release of *The Bands of Mourning*, which came out a few months before *Calamity*. I got to beta read that one as well, so that was the first published Sanderson work that had my name in the acknowledgments, though *Calamity* was the first physical book.

I vividly remember walking into my local indie bookstore on release day, getting my copy of the book, and opening it up to see my name. In print. In a book with Brandon's name on the outside.

That day also ranks up there among the best days of my life.

Calamity was the first book that I started getting the translated editions for. If there was going to be a Sanderson book with my name in it, I was going to have every sparking copy. I ordered the Spanish edition, and was delighted by it.

Things continued to devolve from there until 2018, when I started my YouTube channel, where I called myself The Sanderson Collector. I had been inspired by a book collection from someone known as The Potter Collector, and very much wanted to style myself after him. (This was before JK came out as horrible, and before The Potter Collector switched to posting a bunch of loot boxes and theme park rides instead of books.)

I very much enjoyed making that video, and followed it up with several more. People were actually watching them, and I was starting to accumulate a following. It was here that I made friends with Luke DeProst.

It wasn't too long after this that Mike McDuffie came to me on Facebook and asked about creating a group for collectors. He is a part of the Stephen King collecting community, and wanted to see something similar for the Sanderson community. Together with Luke, we created the Sanderson Collecting group, and it quickly started to grow.

Then in July 2020, soon after COVID hit, Greg Parker created a corresponding Discord server. I quickly joined up, and this became another hub for collectors to meet and chat and share knowledge.

In 2021, Dragonsteel announced their minicon, and invited us to join them as an exhibitor. I personally did not attend that year, because they had very minimal pandemic safety measures in place, and I had a young kid at home who was not yet eligible for the vaccines. However, as a group we decided to attend and host a booth, and have an official name. We were the Sanderson Collectors Guild.

We have had a booth at every Dragonsteel convention since then, and I have attended every year except the first, working long hours and thriving with my community.

In 2021, with Luke, I ran a panel on Brandon Sanderson collecting at JordanCon. JordanCon is a *Wheel of Time* convention that happens every year in Atlanta, GA, and is the closest thing I have to a home. It is a quiet, small convention, but everyone there is amazing. Much of Brandon's fanbase attends, including a large number of beta readers and other avid fans. I count many of these people among my chosen family, and getting to see them every year is the best thing ever. There is no particular single day among these that I would count as a best day of my life, but they're all absolutely amazing. I have a lifetime membership to JordanCon, and intend to keep using it as long as I am, well, alive.

The panel went quite well, with a good attendance for that size of convention. It was well received by the audience, and Luke and I thoroughly enjoyed nerding out about collecting. Luke and I operate very much on the same wavelength, and we tossed together a slide deck and went back and forth about collecting for an hour. We easily could have talked for five, and I personally think we were very engaging and fun.

Two years later, Luke and I applied to run a community panel at Dragonsteel Con 2023. We were accepted, and gave much the same presentation that we had at JordanCon. It was a very well attended panel, and we had a blast doing it. Audience engagement was high, and I had several people tell me that they loved the panel. Maybe in the future I'll get to do something like that again.

During the pandemic, I also started an Instagram page, sharing pictures of my books. I think I've come a long way with those pictures, learning a lot about framing, lighting, and perspective alongside the lessons I've learned about video editing and pacing at the same time. I am very happy with how both my YouTube and Instagram have turned out, and I am very excited to continue learning and improving in both.

I now have thousands of followers/subscribers, and I intend to keep sharing my knowledge and pretty books for years to come, as well as being an active part of the overall collecting community.

Three last tidbits about my time as a collector. The first is my glyph. I am a huge fan of the team that Brandon has accumulated to help him with producing his awesome books. Peter's team on editorial is top notch, and I absolutely adore the artwork that comes from Isaac Stewart's team. At the release party for Starsight, I attended and was volunteering, and had a few spare moments to chat with Isaac. I got him to agree to do a commission piece for me: A glyph that represents me as a collector.

We worked with Peter and established the word "zenef" as the canonical Alethi word for "collector". Isaac then designed an absolutely stunning red-and-black Alethi glyph for me. The glyph says "zenef" in black and "Mark" in red, with the red part reaching down and overlapping the black part, grabbing and collecting it. The glyph took a few years to finalize, but I could not be happier with it. I am eternally in Isaac's debt for creating this amazing art for me. Thank you so much.

The second bit: After the glyph was created, I have had a few friends create things for me based around the glyph. Every single one of these is an absolute treasure that I adore. The one item that I commissioned myself is a custom leatherbound guest book, with my glyph on the spine where the publisher's logo typically goes, that is for my library/museum. I ask everyone who visits now to write me a short note and sign the book, and if someone sends me a book for my collection I ask them to include a note that I can tape into the guest book.

If you're ever in my area, please stop by, see my collection, and sign the book! (Check online for my current location. As of writing, it's near Austin, TX, but that may change in 2025.)

One last tidbit: The truly best day of my life. It is no secret that my favorite character in Brandon's works is Axies the Collector. It's an obvious choice for someone who styles himself as The Sanderson Collector. I have cosplayed Axies on numerous occasions, and to the best of my knowledge I am the only person who has. The last time I asked Brandon about it, I was.

At JordanCon 2021, I got to ask a question at Brandon's Q&A. I asked, "Are we ever going to get more Axies the Collector scenes?". After answering that it was very likely, Brandon then looked at me and said, "Of course, Mark, you would connect with Axies". The whole room broke out laughing. Then he said, "If we need someone to do a cameo [of Axies] if we do a television show, I'll ask them to call you."

So there you have it. I will be Axies the Collector in the *Stormlight* TV show.